D1397422

Thimbleberries®

Quilts for My Sister's House

22 quilting projects for decorating
with flea market finds and collectibles

by

Lynette Jensen

Landauer Books

Thimbleberries®
Quilts *for* My Sister's House

Copyright© 2006 by Landauer Corporation

Projects Copyright© 2006 by Lynette Jensen

This book was designed, produced, and published by Landauer Books
A division of Landauer Corporation
3100 NW 101st Street, Urbandale, Iowa 50322
www.landauercorp.com 800/557-2144

President: Jeramy Lanigan Landauer
Director of Sales & Operations: Kitty Jacobson
Editor-in-Chief: Becky Johnston
Managing Editor: Jeri Simon
Art Director: Laurel Albright
Creative Director: Lynette Jensen
Photographer: Craig Anderson
Photostyling: Lynette Jensen
Technical Writer: Sue Bahr
Technical Illustrator: Lisa Kirchoff

We also wish to thank the support staff of the Thimbleberries® Design Studio:
Sherry Husske, Virginia Brodd, Renae Ashwill, Ardelle Paulson, Julie Jergens, Clarine Howe,
Pearl Baysinger, Tracy Schrantz, Amy Albrecht, and Leone Rusch.

The following manufacturers are licensed to sell Thimbleberries® products:
Thimbleberries® Rugs (www.colonialmills.com);
Thimbleberries® Quilt Stencils (www.quiltingcreations.com);
Thimbleberries® Sewing Thread (www.robison-anton.com); and
Thimbleberries® Fabrics (RJR Fabrics available at independent quilt shops).

Printed in China 10 9 8 7 6 5 4 3 2 1

Library of Congress Cataloging-in-Publication Data
Jensen, Lynette.
  Thimbleberries quilts for my sister's house : 22 quilting projects for
decorating with flea market finds and collectibles / by Lynette Jensen.
        p. cm.
  ISBN-13: 978-1-890621-57-5
  ISBN-10: 1-890621-57-9
1. Patchwork--Patterns. 2. Quilting--Patterns. 3. Interior decoration.
I. Title. II. Title: Quilts for my sister's house.
  TT835.J5245 2006
  746.46'041--dc22

                                                    2006052002
                                    ISBN 10: 1-890621-57-9
                                ISBN 13: 978-1-890621-57-5

Foreword

*Sharing the same affection
for fabric—old or new—*
with my sister, Jan, has been a common bond that
prompted me to surprise her with a collection of quilts
I've designed for Thimbleberries®.

The classic designs blend beautifully with Jan's
southwest-style eclectic furnishings in her snug,
empty-nester home in Colorado Springs that offers a
stunning view of Pike's Peak. These same quilts,
wallhangings, pillows and table toppers are as much
at home in the southwest as they
are in my home and family cabin
on a lake in Minnesota.

I hope you enjoy the results of the
fast-finish decorating shown here
and on the following pages, and
are inspired to gather up your own
collection of family pieces and flea
market finds to accent with quilts
and soft comforts that will be
welcomed by future generations.

My best,

Lynette Jensen

Contents

Decorating with flea market finds and collectibles 8

Quilting Projects 22

Fancy Flywheels Wallhanging 24

Picnic Star Tablecloth 32

Cherry Berry Runner 38

Mini Cherry Berry Runner—Spring 44

Mini Cherry Berry Runner—Autumn 48

Spring Breeze Tablecloth 52

Sugar Maples Throw 56

Spring Garland Quilt 62

Little Brown Bird Pillow 68

Square-in-a-Square Throw 74

Sunshine Patches Throw 80

Blueberries & Cream Quilt 84

Blue House Wallhanging (with Red House alternate) 90

City Block Quilt 96

Summer Lily Quilt 102

Nature Walk Wallhanging 108

Christmas Patches Tablecloth 118

Christmas Bloom Wallhanging 122

Sunshine Porch Quilt 128

Puzzle Perfect Throw 134

Ruffled Pillow Sham 140

Churn Dash Delight Quilt 144

General Instructions 150

Decorating with flea market finds and collectibles

Decorating with flea market finds comes naturally to my sister Jan Koch and to me since many of the well-worn treasures we discover while "antiquing" are the everyday things of our childhood. From flour sack dishtowels, kitchenware, pottery, teapots and enamelware to Mission-style chairs, dressers, and beds, we grew up learning to appreciate the timelessness of pieces of the past that were built to last.

"A little bit of junking" goes a long way to building bridges from our past to our present. Growing up together in a small Minnesota community, Jan and I often spent many pleasant hours with our Dad, Clayton, scouring the surrounding countryside looking for a good deal on a unique chair, table or other toss away. With a little imagination, paint and elbow grease, these ragged rescued pieces were quickly transformed into useful decorative accents for just the right setting in our home.

One of my favorite finds from these rescue missions was a group of three or four tin ceiling panels Dad and Jan picked up in Litchfield that had survived from the fire that burned down the local bakery. Now I've show-cased several of those same panels framed on a shelf above the couch in the family cabin on a lake in Minnesota; Jan uses the tin ceiling panels to add natural texture and tone-on-tone to a kitchen backsplash (shown on page 15) in her home in Colorado; and my daughter Kerry is using a section of that same vintage tin in her bedroom as a wet-wiped black paint accent in her recently restored 1930s-era home.

To this day, when my sister and I get together, we go antiquing. When in Vail, Colorado, for her daughter's wedding, I spotted the cactus lamp shown here that has a southwest feel. It blends with Jan's room coloration, but doesn't dominate in a small space filled with flea market finds like the chest of drawers with the original finish that only needed cleaning and the chocolate brown vintage leather chair and crazy patch pillow.

With "oops" paint and a consignment shop couch, building on traditon with eclectic accents inspired by a classic Churn Dash quilt (featured on page 144) is as easy as one, two, three.

Start by painting walls and ceiling in neutral shades of what my sister Jan, calls her "oops" paint. Jan routinely visits the local hardware store on a mission to find cans of mixed paint that were someone else's mistake and her opportunity to make it work in the desert neutrals of her southwest decorating style. Jan used the marked-down "oops" paint to "marry" similar styles of wall units for displaying her collection of Red Wing vases and other ceramic pottery. The final touch is a contemporary leather couch from the consignment shop that is sized right for the small room and almost a perfect match for the "oops" paint on the wall.

Anything goes, if you make it your own. In my sister's house, Jan has a knack for bringing it all together—from top to bottom.

The ceiling paint is tonal and contrasts with the pottery Jan displays by color on the country wardrobe surrounded by children's chairs and table and the Spring Garland quilt. The distressed faux mantel covered with pressed tin offers texture as does the lamp base. Personal touches include several of the Andrew Wyeth watercolor prints Jan has collected from the 17 years she lived "just down the road" from this well-known American artist in Chadd's Ford, Pennsylvania.

Adding color with dried flowers is a decorating detail that both Jan and I have discovered works for almost any budget. The larger your cutting garden, the more generous your bouquet will be.

We seldom pass up the opportunity to dry flowers and blooms from our gardens to display in both new and old blended pottery from our ever-growing collections of flea market finds.

From nightstand to wine rack— in no time at all. Jan's husband, Don, cleverly transformed a clunky old nightstand into a modified wine storage unit by simply adding shelves and a door and tying it all together with a coat of whitewash paint rubbed and distressed to add a weathered southwest-style flavor.

Jan and Don also added southwest texture and style by choosing Saltee ceramic tile for the floor. The tile adds texture, terra-cotta color, unifies the space between the kitchen and living area, and works well with both antique and found pieces.

Beauty in the bath begins with plenty of storage that does double duty for displays of pieces from the past. My sister Jan took the plunge by tearing out the dated sink cabinet and replacing it with a flea market dresser and a chest that she prefers over a linen closet. Both offer generous surfaces for collectibles. "Oops" paint, an ice cream parlor chair, and framed photos taken by her son Michael are reflected in the mirror to complete the picture.

Same design but different sizes and colors provide greater impact for a grouping of collectible teapots shown at left.

Jan's birthday is in August and through the years she and her family have returned to Minnesota for family gatherings. Finding pottery and a teapot or two to add to her collection has been my special birthday treat for Jan.

Collecting the style of pottery shown below has been a favorite pastime for Jan for many years. As her pottery collection grows, so does the need for additional display space. This creates a delightful dilemma for a dedicated collector—adding more cupboards that need to be filled.

For small space decorating, every surface counts and Jan has discovered how to take advantage of "found" space for her "found" collectibles. At left, when not in use, the stove top provides surface for storage and display of serving pieces and collectibles—from a ceramic rooster to a painted metal tray (all are heat-resistant). One of the tin ceiling panels that Dad and Jan salvaged from the bakery that burned down in Litchfield years ago, is painted and pressed into service as an obviously fireproof backsplash.

The island, below left, is covered with pieces of tile salvaged from floor installation and the two "found" stained glass pieces propped up on the windowsill below, serve as a serene backsplash for potted plants.

Long on collectibles, short on space is a common cause of frustration for folks like Jan who go out for a "little bit of junking" and come back with a truckful of treasures. My sister's house is a tribute to Jan's ingenuity and unique gift for using salvaged architectural elements for decorating details. In the kitchen, Jan has added vintage cupboard doors to the wall to use as a textured display background and used a weathered porch post to frame the doorway. To brighten the desert tones of southwest-style decorating and complement the white kitchen appliances and trim, Jan collects white pottery of the McCoy, Bauer and Shawnee variety and specializes in finding unique ways to display it. She piles imperfect or mismatched pieces into a centerpiece basket on a quilt covered tabletop. The Spring Breeze quilt with complete instructions is featured on page 52.

Sweeten it with butter cream

and discover the difference between plain vanilla and buttery soft accents throughout the room.

In the photo at right, Jan's eye for detail adds depth to the room by starting with the butter cream lamp in the living room accompanied by a fresh bouquet of yellow blooms that takes the viewer's eye down the hall to a grouping of found artwork in mismatched frames. Often framed "found" prints from the forties or paintings by amateur artists are more interesting than priceless paintings—and the price is right.

The ruffled pillow and table runner are featured with complete instructions on pages 140 and 44.

Grandmother's rag bag

is often overlooked as an excellent source for recycling wornout clothing.

Over the years, Jan and I have each found unusual ways to use the rag balls from our grandmother's rug weaving room. In earlier times, men wore striped denim overalls for farm chores. When a pair of overalls finally wore out, grandmother would cut the side seams and roll them up into carpet rag balls to make rugs. Jan used muslin strips and those denim overall rag balls to weave a new back and seat for a relic rocker (shown at left in detail). At right, an old trellis holds flowers for drying and enamel colanders. The Picnic Star Tablecloth draped on the chair is featured on page 32.

Finding space for found objects can be a challenge in a an empty-nester's downsized home. In the narrow hall, above, the best way to go is up.

Jan trimmed out a plain bookcase with wooden slats and painted it barn red for greater contrast with her stunning collection of whiteware topped off by a framed print.

Almost anything goes in an eclectic setting with a southwest-style flavor accented with everything from art deco to Mission.

In my sister's bedroom, Jan was able to artfully arrange an amazing collection of diverse styles and make it all blend beautifully. The chair at left is Mission-style with an antique bark cloth pillow in a bold floral print that coordinates with the green leather chair seat. An iron piano stool transitions to a side table.

At top right, a vintage screen door backed with fabric stretched on curtain rods is attached by hinges to a box with shelves Jan's husband made from scrap wood. He also built a solid wooden footboard and headboard for the bed with parts of salvaged fence gates. The wide pine floor planks are also salvaged.

Bed springs are eternal when recycled into a metal basket sculpture surrounded by stars that my sister Jan fondly refers to as "my spring garden."

Other interesting found objects include the newly purchased multi-pointed metal star, top left, and silo shoots used as plant stands, above, and paired with a galvanized watering can accent piece.

Other long-lasting metal mementos are the waffle irons (the heart-shaped one is from my childhood playhouse) and other iron gear arranged in a terra-cotta pot to resemble a cactus.

The stars are out tonight and every night in this dramatic bedroom setting with an eight-pointed star used as wall art. Inexpensive, but impressive, the wall is painted in tonals and beiges and coordinates handsomely with the City Block quilt and pillows on the bed shown below. The quilt is offered as a project with instructions on page 96.

Quilting Projects

*Flywheel blocks take on a southwest flavor
when worked in terra-cotta and earth-tone fabric prints.
The scalloped border appliqué adds interest.*

Fancy Flywheels

Wallhanging

45-inches square

Fabrics and Supplies

1 yard **LARGE GREEN/ROSE FLORAL**
for block centers and outer border

7/8 yard **GOLD PRINT**
for blocks and scalloped border

1/4 yard **ROSE PRINT** for blocks

1/2 yard **BEIGE PRINT** for blocks

1 yard **DARK GREEN PRINT**
for blocks, lattice post squares, corner
blocks, and scalloped border binding

2/3 yard **RED FLORAL**
for lattice segments and corner blocks

1/2 yard **DARK GREEN PRINT** for binding

3 yards for backing

quilt batting, 51-inches square

freezer paper for scalloped border appliqué

Pieced Blocks

Makes 4 blocks

Cutting

From **LARGE GREEN/ROSE FLORAL:**
- Cut 1, 3-1/2 x 17-inch strip

From **GOLD PRINT:**
- Cut 2, 2 x 17-inch strips
- Cut 2, 2 x 42-inch strips. From the strips cut:
  8, 2 x 6-1/2-inch rectangles

From **ROSE PRINT:**
- Cut 1, 3-7/8 x 42-inch strip

From **BEIGE PRINT:**
- Cut 1, 3-7/8 x 42-inch strip
- Cut 2, 3-1/2 x 42-inch strips. From the strips cut:
  16, 3-1/2-inch squares

From **DARK GREEN PRINT:**
- Cut 2, 3-1/2 x 42-inch strips. From the strips cut:
  16, 3-1/2-inch squares

Piecing

Step 1 Aligning long edges, sew the 2 x 17-inch **GOLD** strips to both side edges of the 3-1/2 x 17-inch **LARGE GREEN/ROSE FLORAL** strip. Press, referring to *Hints and Helps for Pressing Strip Sets* on page 158.

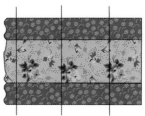

Cut 4, 3-1/2-inch wide segments

Step 2 Referring to the block diagram, sew 2 x 6-1/2-inch **GOLD** rectangles to the side edges of a Step 1 segment; press. Make 4 block centers. <u>At this point each block center should measure 6-1/2-inches square.</u>

Step 3 With right sides together, layer the 3-7/8 x 42-inch **ROSE** and **BEIGE** strips together. Press together, but do not sew. Cut the layered strips into squares. Cut the layered squares in half diagonally to make 16 sets of triangles. Stitch 1/4-inch from the diagonal edge of each pair of triangles; press.

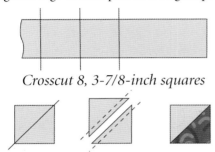

Crosscut 8, 3-7/8-inch squares

Make 16, 3-1/2-inch triangle-pieced squares

Step 4 Sew a 3-1/2-inch **DARK GREEN** square to the left edge of each triangle-pieced square; press. Make 16 units. Referring to the block diagram, sew 2 of the units to the top/bottom edges of each block center; press.

Make 16

Step 5 Sew 3-1/2-inch **BEIGE** squares to both ends of each of the remaining Step 4 units; press. Sew the units to both side edges of the Step 4 units; press. <u>At this point each block should measure 12-1/2-inches square.</u>

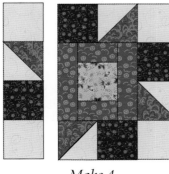

Make 4

Quilt Center

Cutting

From **RED FLORAL**:
- Cut 4, 3-1/2 x 42-inch strips. From the strips cut: 12, 3-1/2 x 12-1/2-inch lattice segments

From **DARK GREEN PRINT**:
- Cut 1, 3-1/2 x 42-inch strip. From the strip cut: 9, 3-1/2-inch lattice post squares

Quilt Center Assembly

Step 1 Referring to the quilt diagram for placement, sew together 2 of the pieced blocks and 3 of the 3-1/2 x 12-1/2-inch **RED FLORAL** lattice segments. Press the seam allowances toward the lattice segments. Make 2 block rows.

Step 2 Sew together 2 of the 3-1/2 x 12-1/2-inch **RED FLORAL** lattice segments and 3 of the 3-1/2-inch **DARK GREEN** lattice post squares. Press the seam allowances toward the lattice segments. Make 3 lattice strips.

Step 3 Pin the block rows and the lattice strips together at the block intersections; sew. Press the seam allowances in one direction. <u>At this point the quilt center should measure 33-1/2-inches square.</u>

Borders

Note: *The yardage given allows for the border strips to be cut on the crosswise grain.*

Cutting

From **LARGE GREEN/ROSE FLORAL**:
- Cut 4, 6-1/2 x 42-inch outer border strips

From **GOLD PRINT**:
- Cut 4, 5 x 42-inch strips for scalloped border

From **RED FLORAL**:
- Cut 2, 2 x 42-inch strips. From the strips cut: 8, 2 x 6-1/2-inch rectangles for corner block borders
- Cut 2, 2 x 17-inch strips

From **DARK GREEN PRINT:**
- Cut 1, 3-1/2 x 17-inch strip
- Cut enough 1-3/4-inch wide **bias** strips to make 4, 37-inch long binding strips

From freezer paper:
- Cut 1 Pattern A for scalloped border.
The freezer paper can be reused.

Assembling and Attaching the Borders

Step 1   Aligning long edges, sew the 2 x 17-inch **RED FLORAL** strips to both side edges of the 3-1/2 x 17-inch **DARK GREEN** strip; press. Crosscut the strip set into segments.

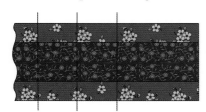

Cut 4, 3-1/2-inch wide segments

Step 2   Referring to the corner block diagram, sew 2 x 6-1/2-inch **RED FLORAL** rectangles to both side edges of each Step 1 segment; press. <u>At this point each corner block should measure 6-1/2-inches square.</u>

Make 4

Prepare and Appliqué the Scalloped Border

Step 1   Make a freezer paper template of Scalloped Border Pattern A on pages 29 and 30.

Step 2   Aligning straight edges, lay the freezer paper Pattern A, coated side down, on the wrong side of a 5 x 42-inch **GOLD** strip. With a hot, dry iron, press the freezer paper template in place. Cut out the scalloped border using the freezer paper scalloped edge as your cutting guide. Remove the freezer paper and use it as a guide to cut 3 more scalloped borders.

Step 3   Aligning straight raw edges, position the scalloped borders on the 6-1/2 x 42-inch **LARGE GREEN/ROSE FLORAL** outer border strips. Stitch a scant 1/4-inch from the raw scalloped edge of the **GOLD** scalloped border.

Step 4   Cut away the **LARGE GREEN/ROSE FLORAL** outer border that falls behind the **GOLD** overlay. To do so, turn the prepared border strip over and cut 1/4-inch beyond the stitching line, creating a 1/4-inch seam allowance. This eliminates the double thickness of fabric otherwise created by this scalloped border.

Note: An appliqué scissors is very helpful for cutting away the excess outer border fabric.

Step 5   For each border, fold a 1-3/4-inch wide **DARK GREEN** bias strip in half lengthwise, wrong sides together; press. Referring to the diagram, lay the bias strip on the scalloped edge of the **GOLD** border, having raw edges even.

Step 6   Stitch a 1/4-inch from the raw scalloped edge. As you stitch, gently ease the binding onto the curved edge. This will prevent the scalloped edges from "cupping." This happens when the binding is stretched as it is sewn on.

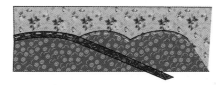

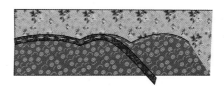

Step 7 At the inside point of the scallops, with your needle in the down position, raise your presser foot so that you can maneuver the border and binding. Realign the raw edges, lower the presser foot, and continue stitching. With the tip of a pin or needle, push the edge of the binding strip, making sure it continues to meet the edge of the scallop. This will create a small amount of fullness in the binding at the pivot points, which will be concealed when the folded edge of the binding is hand stitched in place.

Step 8 Fold the binding strip over to cover the raw edges; hand stitch the binding in place. At the point of each scallop "dip" a small fold will be created as in mitering binding corners. Press and hand tack this area to keep it flat. Trim the prepared border strips to 33-1/2-inches long (or to the measurement of your quilt center).

Step 9 Attach a prepared border strip to the top/bottom edges of the quilt center; press. Sew the prepared 6-1/2-inch corner blocks to both ends of the remaining prepared border strips; press. Attach the border strips to the side edges of the quilt center; press.

Putting It All Together

Cut the 3 yard length of backing fabric in half crosswise to make 2, 1-1/2 yard lengths. Refer to *Finishing the Quilt* on page 159 for complete instructions.

Quilting Suggestions:

• Lattice segments - TB27 Heart Vine Border.

• Pieced blocks - TB10 Radish Top.

*The **THIMBLEBERRIES**® quilt stencils are by Quilting Creations International.*

Binding

Cutting

From **DARK GREEN PRINT**:
• Cut 5, 2-3/4 x 42-inch strips

Sew the binding to the quilt using a 3/8-inch seam allowance. This measurement will produce a 1/2-inch wide finished double binding. Refer to *Binding* and *Diagonal Piecing* on page 159 for complete instructions.

TB27 Heart Vine Border Quilting Suggestion

TB10 Radish Top Quilting Suggestion

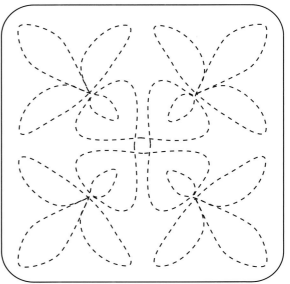

Upper Scallop Unit

*To make the Scallop Border Pattern A, match the Upper Scallop Unit to the
Lower Scallop Unit (on page 30) along the dashed lines*

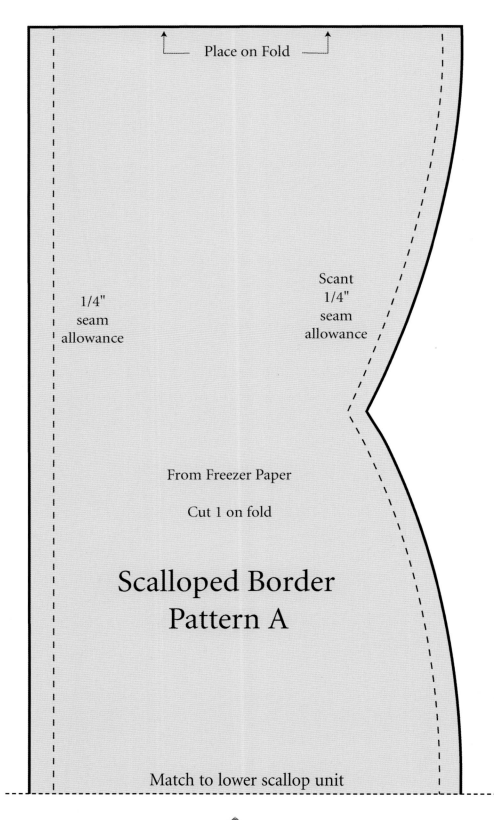

Place on Fold

1/4"
seam
allowance

Scant
1/4"
seam
allowance

From Freezer Paper

Cut 1 on fold

Scalloped Border
Pattern A

Match to lower scallop unit

Lower Scallop Unit

To make the Scallop Border Pattern A, match the Lower Scallop Unit to the Upper Scallop Unit (on page 29) along the dashed lines

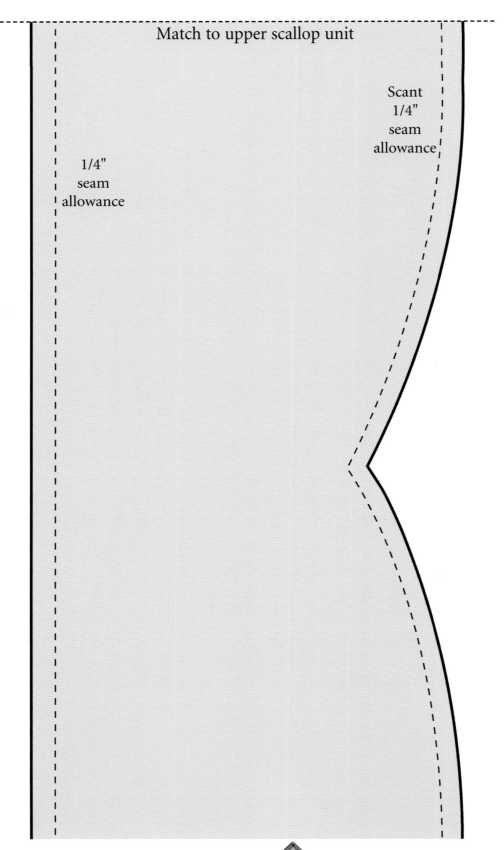

Match to upper scallop unit

Scant
1/4"
seam
allowance

1/4"
seam
allowance

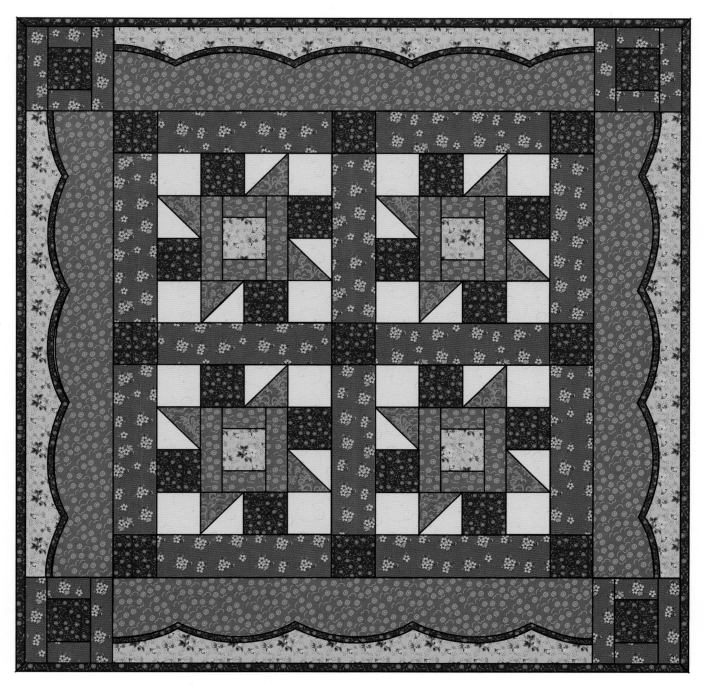

Fancy Flywheels Wallhanging
45-inches square

Traditional quilt blocks were often named for natural surroundings. For the early pioneers who traversed the southwestern desert terrain at night to avoid the heat, the eight-pointed star is a visual reminder of the evening sky.

Picnic Star

Tablecloth

58-inches square

Fabrics and Supplies

1-2/3 yards **GREEN FLORAL**
for star and outer border

5/8 yard **BEIGE PRINT #1**
for star background

1/4 yard **DARK GREEN PRINT**
for first inner border

3/8 yard **ROSE PRINT**
for second inner border

3/4 yard **MEDIUM GREEN PRINT**
for checkerboard units
and second middle border

7/8 yard **BEIGE PRINT #2**
for checkerboard border

1/3 yard **GOLD PRINT**
for first middle border

2/3 yard **ROSE PRINT** for binding

3-3/4 yards for backing

quilt batting, at least 64-inches square

Star Block

Cutting

From **GREEN FLORAL:**
- Cut 1, 9-1/4 x 42-inch strip. From the strip cut:
  2, 9-1/4-inch squares
  1, 8-1/2-inch center square

From **BEIGE PRINT #1:**
- Cut 1, 9-1/4 x 42-inch strip. From the strip cut:
  2, 9-1/4-inch squares
- Cut 1, 8-1/2 x 42-inch strip. From the strip cut:
  4, 8-1/2-inch squares

Piecing

Step 1 With right sides together, layer the 9-1/4-inch **GREEN FLORAL** and **BEIGE #1** squares in pairs. Cut the layered squares diagonally into quarters to make 8 triangle sets.

Make 8 triangle sets

Step 2 Stitch along the bias edge of a triangle set being careful not to stretch the triangles; press. Repeat this process with the remaining triangle sets, stitching along the same bias edge of each to make a triangle unit. Sew the triangle units together in pairs to make the hourglass units; press. At this point each hourglass unit should measure 8-1/2-inches square.

Bias edges

Make 8 triangle units

Make 4 hourglass units

Step 3 Referring to the quilt diagram for placement, lay out the hourglass units, the 4, 8-1/2-inch **BEIGE #1** squares, and the 8-1/2-inch **GREEN FLORAL** center square. Sew together the squares in each row. Press the seam allowances away from the hourglass units. Sew together the rows; press. At this point the star block should measure 24-1/2-inches square.

Inner Borders

*Note: The yardage given allows for the border strips to be cut on the crosswise grain. Diagonally piece the strips as needed, referring to **Diagonal Piecing** instructions on page 159. Read through **Border** instructions on page 158 for general instructions on adding borders.*

Cutting

From **DARK GREEN PRINT:**
   • Cut 4, 1-1/2 x 42-inch first inner border strips

From **ROSE PRINT:**
   • Cut 4, 2-1/2 x 42-inch second inner border strips

Attaching the Inner Borders

Step 1 Attach the 1-1/2-inch wide **DARK GREEN** first inner border strips.

Step 2 Attach the 2-1/2-inch wide **ROSE** second inner border strips.

Checkerboard Borders

Cutting

From **MEDIUM GREEN PRINT:**
   • Cut 5, 2-1/2 x 42-inch strips

From **BEIGE PRINT #2:**
   • Cut 2, 6-1/2 x 42-inch strips. From the strips cut:
   4, 6-1/2 x 10-1/2-inch rectangles
   4, 6-1/2-inch squares
   • Cut 4, 2-1/2 x 42-inch strips

Piecing

Step 1 Aligning long edges, sew 2 of the 2-1/2 x 42-inch **MEDIUM GREEN** strips to both side edges of a 2-1/2 x 42-inch **BEIGE #2** strip. Press the seam allowances toward the **MEDIUM GREEN** strips referring to **Hints and Helps for Pressing Strip Sets** on page 35. Make 2 strip sets. Cut the strip sets into segments.

Crosscut 24, 2-1/2-inch wide segments

Step 2 Aligning long edges sew 2 of the 2-1/2 x 42-inch **BEIGE #2** strips to both side edges of a 2-1/2 x 42-inch **MEDIUM GREEN** strip; press. Make 1 strip set. Cut the strip set into segments.

Crosscut 16, 2-1/2-inch wide segments

Step 3 Sew together 3 of the Step 1 segments and 2 of the Step 2 segments; press. At this point each checkerboard unit should measure 6-1/2 x 10-1/2-inches.

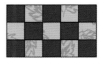

Make 8 checkerboard units

Step 4 Sew checkerboard units to both side edges of a 6-1/2 x 10-1/2-inch **BEIGE #2** rectangle; press. Make 4 checkerboard borders. At this point each border strip should measure 6-1/2 x 30-1/2-inches. Sew 2 of the checkerboard borders to the top/bottom edges of the quilt center.

Make 4

Step 5 Sew 6-1/2-inch **BEIGE #2** squares to both side edges of the remaining checkerboard borders; press. Sew the checkerboard borders to the side edges of the quilt center; press. <u>At this point the quilt center should measure 42-1/2-inches square.</u>

Middle and Outer Borders

*Note: The yardage given allows for the border strips to be cut on the crosswise grain. Diagonally piece the strips as needed, referring to **Diagonal Piecing** instructions on page 159. Read through **Border** instructions on page 158 for general instructions on adding borders.*

Cutting

From **GOLD PRINT:**
  • Cut 5, 1-1/2 x 42-inch first middle border strips

From **MEDIUM GREEN PRINT:**
  • Cut 6, 1-1/2 x 42-inch second middle border strips

From **GREEN FLORAL:**
  • Cut 7, 6-1/2 x 42-inch outer border strips

Attaching the Middle and Outer Borders

Step 1 Attach the 1-1/2-inch wide **GOLD** first middle border strips.

Step 2 Attach the 1-1/2-inch wide **MEDIUM GREEN** second middle border strips.

Step 3 Attach the 6-1/2-inch wide **GREEN FLORAL** outer border strips.

Putting It All Together

Cut the 3-3/4 yard length of backing fabric in half crosswise to make 2, 1-7/8 yard lengths. Refer to *Finishing the Quilt* on page 159 for complete instructions.

Binding

Cutting

From **ROSE PRINT:**
  • Cut 7, 2-3/4 x 42-inch strips

Sew the binding to the quilt using a 3/8-inch seam allowance. This measurement will produce a 1/2-inch wide finished double binding. Refer to ***Binding*** and ***Diagonal Piecing*** on page 159 for complete instructions.

Hints and Helps for Pressing Strip Sets

When sewing strips of fabric together for strip sets, it is important to press the seam allowances nice and flat, usually to the dark fabric. Be careful not to stretch as you press, causing a "rainbow effect." This will affect the accuracy and shape of the pieces cut from the strip set. Press on the wrong side first with the strips perpendicular to the ironing board. Flip the piece over and press on the right side to prevent little pleats from forming at the seams. Laying the strip set lengthwise on the ironing board seems to encourage the rainbow effect.

Avoid this rainbow effect

*The green, rust and rose fabrics in Picnic Stars blend beautifully with
the backdrop of vibrant roses on an old trellis used as a drying rack.
The trellis also offers plenty of parking space for a collection of vintage enamel colanders.*

Picnic Star Tablecloth

58-inches square

*What could be more cheerful than a tabletop covered with appliquéd
cherry berry blossoms? The pattern is an easy repeat
for making multiples of leaves, stems and berries.*

Cherry Berry

Runner

30 x 50-inches

Fabrics and Supplies

1/4 yard **RED PRINT**
for runner center and berry appliqués

5/8 yard **GREEN PRINT**
for runner center and leaf/stem appliqués

1-1/4 yards **BEIGE PRINT**
for background and outer border

1/4 yard **TAN PRINT** for inner border

1/2 yard **GREEN/BLACK PLAID**
for binding (cut on the bias)

1-5/8 yards for backing

quilt batting, at least 36 x 56-inches

freezer paper for leaf appliqués

3-inch square of lightweight cardboard
for circle appliqués

Runner Center

Cutting

From **RED PRINT**:
- Cut 2, 2-1/2 x 42-inch strips. From the strips cut:
  25, 2-1/2-inch squares

From **GREEN PRINT**:
- Cut 2, 2-1/2 x 42-inch strips. From the strips cut:
  24, 2-1/2-inch squares

From **BEIGE PRINT**:
- Cut 1, 4-1/2 x 42-inch strip. From the strip cut:
  2, 4-1/2 x 14-1/2-inch rectangles
- Cut 3, 2-1/2 x 42-inch strips. From the strips cut:
  2, 2-1/2 x 10-1/2-inch rectangles
  6, 2-1/2 x 6-1/2-inch rectangles
  4, 2-1/2 x 4-1/2-inch rectangles
  6, 2-1/2-inch squares

Piecing

Step 1 Referring to the diagram for placement, lay out 8 of the **RED** squares, 4 of the **GREEN** squares, 1 of the **BEIGE** squares, 1 of the 2-1/2 x 6-1/2-inch **BEIGE** rectangles, and 1 of the 2-1/2 x 10-1/2-inch **BEIGE** rectangles to make the top/bottom sections. Sew the pieces together in each row. Press the seam allowances in alternating directions by rows so the seams will fit snugly together with less bulk. Sew the rows together; press. At this point the top/bottom sections should measure 6-1/2 x 14-1/2-inches.

Make 2

Step 2 Referring to the diagram for placement, lay out the remaining **RED**, **GREEN**, and **BEIGE** squares and rectangles to make the center section. Sew the pieces together in each row. Press the seam allowances in alternating directions by rows. Sew the rows together; press. At this point the center section should measure 14-1/2-inches square.

Make 1

Step 3 Referring to the runner center assembly diagram, sew the 4-1/2 x 14-1/2-inch **BEIGE** rectangles to the top/bottom edges of the center section; press. Sew the top/bottom sections to the edges of the runner center section; press. At this point the runner center should measure 14-1/2 x 34-1/2-inches.

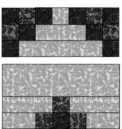

Make 1

Borders

*Note: The yardage given allows for the border strips to be cut on the crosswise grain. Diagonally piece the strips as needed, referring to **Diagonal Piecing** instructions on page 159. Read through **Border** instructions on page 158 for general instructions on adding borders.*

Cutting

From **TAN PRINT**:
- Cut 3, 2-1/2 x 42-inch inner border strips

From **BEIGE PRINT**:
- Cut 4, 6-1/2 x 42-inch outer border strips

Attaching the Borders

Step 1 Attach the 2-1/2-inch wide **TAN** inner border strips.

Step 2 Attach the 6-1/2-inch wide **BEIGE** outer border strips.

Appliqué

Cutting

From **GREEN PRINT:**

- Cut 2, 1-3/8 x 14-inch **bias** strips for stems for quilt center
- Cut 4, 1-3/8 x 9-inch **bias** strips for stems for border

Prepare the Stems

Step 1 To make each stem, fold a 1-3/8-inch wide **GREEN** strip in half lengthwise with wrong sides together; press. To keep the raw edges aligned, stitch a scant 1/4-inch away from the edges. Fold the strip in half again so the raw edges are hidden by the first folded edge; press. Repeat to prepare all the stems.

Step 2 Referring to the quilt diagram for placement, position the prepared stems on the runner top; hand baste or pin in place.

Prepare the Leaf Appliqués — Freezer Paper Appliqué Method

With this method of hand appliqué, the freezer paper forms a base around which the leaf appliqués are shaped. The circular berry shapes will be appliquéd using the cardboard appliqué method.

Step 1 Make a template using the shape on page 42. With a pencil, trace the shape on the dull side of the freezer paper the number of times indicated on the pattern. Cut out the shapes on the traced lines.

Step 2 With a hot, dry iron, press the coated side of each freezer paper shape onto the wrong side of the fabric chosen for the appliqués. Allow at least 1/2-inch between each shape for seam allowances. Cut out each shape a scant 1/4-inch beyond the edge of the freezer paper pattern.

Step 3 Referring to the runner diagram, position and pin the leaf appliqué shapes to the runner top.

Step 4 With your needle, turn the seam allowances over the edge of the freezer paper and hand appliqué the leaves in place. When there is about 3/4-inch left to appliqué, slide your needle into this opening, loosen the freezer paper from the fabric, and gently pull the freezer paper out. Finish stitching the appliqué in place. Hand appliqué the stems in place.

Prepare the Berry Appliqués — Cardboard Appliqué Method

Step 1 Make a cardboard template using the berry pattern on page 42.

Step 2 Position the berry template on the wrong side of the fabric chosen for the appliqué and trace around the template 42 times, leaving a 3/4-inch margin around each shape. Remove the template and cut a scant 1/4-inch beyond the drawn lines.

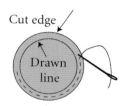

Step 3 To create smooth, round circles, run a line of basting stitches around each circle, placing the stitches halfway between the drawn line and the cut edge of the circle. After basting, keep the needle and thread attached for the next step.

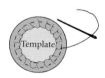

Step 4 Place the cardboard template on the wrong side of the fabric circle and tug on the basting stitches, gathering the fabric over the template. When the thread is tight, space the gathers evenly, and make a knot to secure the thread. Clip the thread, press the circle, and remove the cardboard template. Continue this process to make 42 berries.

Step 5 Hand appliqué the berries with matching thread, covering the ends of the stems as needed.

Putting It All Together

Trim the backing and batting so they are 6-inches larger than the runner top. Refer to *Finishing the Quilt* on page 159 for complete instructions.

Binding

Cutting

From **GREEN/BLACK PLAID:**
- Cut enough 2-3/4-inch wide **bias** strips to total 170-inches

Sew the binding to the quilt using a 3/8-inch seam allowance. This measurement will produce a 1/2-inch wide finished double binding. Refer to *Binding* and *Diagonal Piecing* on page 159 for complete instructions.

Leaf
Trace 18 onto
freezer paper

Berry
Trace onto
lightweight
cardboard

Cherry Berry Runner
30 x 50-inches

Spring into summer with a mini cherry berry table runner that radiates the beauty of the season. Easy piecing makes this a quick pick-me-up.

Cherry Berry

Spring

Runner

15 x 25-inches

Fabrics and Supplies

1/8 yard **YELLOW PRINT** for runner center

1/8 yard **LIGHT ROSE PRINT** for runner center squares

1/4 yard **BEIGE PRINT** for background

1/8 yard **GREEN PRINT** for inner border

1/4 yard **DARK ROSE PRINT** for outer border

1/4 yard **GREEN PRINT** for binding

5/8 yard for backing

quilt batting, at least 21 x 31-inches

Runner Center

Cutting

From **YELLOW PRINT:**
- Cut 1, 1-1/2 x 42-inch strip. From the strip cut: 25, 1-1/2-inch squares

From **LIGHT ROSE PRINT:**
- Cut 1, 1-1/2 x 42-inch strip. From the strip cut: 24, 1-1/2-inch squares

From **BEIGE PRINT:**
- Cut 1, 2-1/2 x 42-inch strip. From the strip cut:
  2, 2-1/2 x 7-1/2-inch rectangles
  2, 1-1/2 x 5-1/2-inch rectangles
- Cut 1, 1-1/2 x 42-inch strip. From the strip cut:
  6, 1-1/2 x 3-1/2-inch rectangles
  4, 1-1/2 x 2-1/2-inch rectangles
  6, 1-1/2-inch squares

Piecing

Step 1 Referring to the diagram for placement, lay out 8 of the **YELLOW** squares, 4 of the **LIGHT ROSE** squares, 1 of the **BEIGE** squares, 1 of the 1-1/2 x 3-1/2-inch **BEIGE** rectangles, and 1 of the 1-1/2 x 5-1/2-inch **BEIGE** rectangles to make the top/bottom sections. Sew the pieces together in each row. Press the seam allowances in alternating directions by rows so the seams will fit snugly together with less bulk. Sew the rows together; press. Sew a 2-1/2 x 7-1/2-inch **BEIGE** rectangle to the bottom edge of the unit; press. Make 2 sections. At this point each top/bottom section should measure 5-1/2 x 7-1/2-inches.

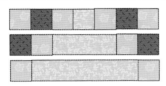

Make 2

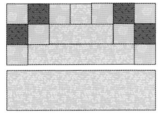

Make 2

Step 2 Referring to the diagram for placement, lay out the remaining **YELLOW**, **LIGHT ROSE**, and **BEIGE** squares and rectangles to make the center section. Sew the pieces together in each row. Press the seam allowances in alternating directions by rows. Sew the rows together; press. At this point the center section should measure 7-1/2-inches square.

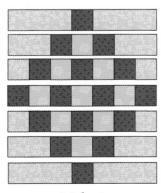

Make 1

Step 3 Sew the top/bottom sections to the top/bottom edges of the center section; press. At this point the runner center should measure 7-1/2 x 17-1/2-inches.

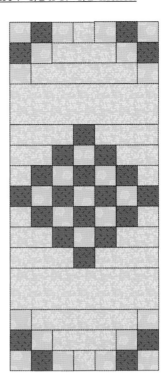

Borders

*Note: The yardage given allows for the border strips to be cut on the crosswise grain. Read through **Border** instructions on page 158 for general instructions on adding borders.*

Cutting

From GREEN PRINT:

- Cut 2, 1-1/2 x 42-inch inner border strips

From DARK ROSE PRINT:

- Cut 2, 3-1/2 x 42-inch outer border strips

Attaching the Borders

Step 1 Attach the 1-1/2-inch wide **GREEN** inner border strips.

Step 2 Attach the 3-1/2-inch wide **DARK ROSE PRINT** outer border strips.

Putting It All Together

Trim the backing and batting so they are 6-inches larger than the runner top. Refer to **Finishing the Quilt** on page 159 for complete instructions.

Binding

Cutting

From **GREEN PRINT:**

• Cut 3, 2-3/4 x 42-inch strips

Sew the binding to the quilt using a 3/8-inch seam allowance. This measurement will produce a 1/2-inch wide finished double binding. Refer to **Binding** and **Diagonal Piecing** on page 159 for complete instructions.

Mini Cherry Berry — Spring Runner
15 x 25-inches

Autumn leaves are falling into place on this table runner designed to be a fast-finish decorating accent for the harvest table.

Mini
Cherry Berry
Autumn

Runner

15 x 25-inches

Fabrics and Supplies

1/8 yard **ORANGE PRINT**
for runner center squares

1/8 yard **BLACK PRINT**
for runner center squares

1/4 yard **BEIGE PRINT** for background

1/8 yard **GREEN PRINT** for inner border

1/4 yard **RED/GOLD LEAF PRINT**
for outer border

1/4 yard **BLACK DIAGONAL PRINT**
for binding

5/8 yard for backing

quilt batting, at least 21 x 31-inches

Runner Center

Cutting

From **ORANGE PRINT**:
- Cut 1, 1-1/2 x 42-inch strip. From the strip cut:
  25, 1-1/2-inch squares

From **BLACK PRINT**:
- Cut 1, 1-1/2 x 42-inch strip. From the strip cut:
  24, 1-1/2-inch squares

From **BEIGE PRINT**:
- Cut 1, 2-1/2 x 42-inch strip. From the strip cut:
  2, 2-1/2 x 7-1/2-inch rectangles
  2, 1-1/2 x 5-1/2-inch rectangles
- Cut 1, 1-1/2 x 42-inch strip. From the strip cut:
  6, 1-1/2 x 3-1/2-inch rectangles
  4, 1-1/2 x 2-1/2-inch rectangles
  6, 1-1/2-inch squares

Piecing

Step 1 Referring to the diagram for placement, lay out 8 of the **ORANGE** squares, 4 of the **BLACK** squares, 1 of the **BEIGE** squares, 1 of the 1-1/2 x 3-1/2-inch **BEIGE** rectangles, and 1 of the 1-1/2 x 5-1/2-inch **BEIGE** rectangles to make the top/bottom sections. Sew the pieces together in each row. Press the seam allowances in alternating directions by rows so the seams will fit snugly together with less bulk. Sew the rows together; press. Sew a 2-1/2 x 7-1/2-inch **BEIGE** rectangle to the bottom edge of the unit; press. Make 2 sections. At this point each top/bottom section should measure 5-1/2 x 7-1/2-inches.

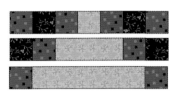

Make 2

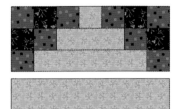

Make 2

Step 2 Referring to the diagram for placement, lay out the remaining **ORANGE**, **BLACK**, and **BEIGE** squares and rectangles to make the center section. Sew the pieces together in each row. Press the seam allowances in alternating directions by rows. Sew the rows together; press. At this point the center section should measure 7-1/2-inches square.

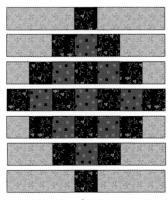

Make 1

Step 3 Sew the top/bottom sections to the top/bottom edges of the center section; press. At this point the runner center should measure 7-1/2 x 17-1/2-inches.

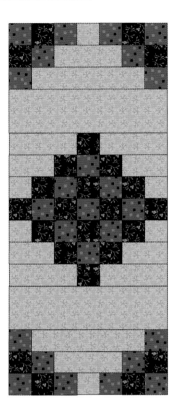

Borders

Note: *The yardage given allows for the border strips to be cut on the crosswise grain. Read through* **Border** *instructions on page 158 for general instructions on adding borders.*

Cutting

From **GREEN PRINT:**

• Cut 2, 1-1/2 x 42-inch inner border strips

From **RED/GOLD LEAF PRINT:**

• Cut 2, 3-1/2 x 42-inch outer border strips

Attaching the Borders

Step 1 Attach the 1-1/2-inch wide **GREEN** inner border strips.

Step 2 Attach the 3-1/2-inch wide **RED/GOLD LEAF PRINT** outer border strips.

Putting It All Together

Trim the backing and batting so they are 6-inches larger than the runner top. Refer to *Finishing the Quilt* on page 159 for complete instructions.

Binding

Cutting

From **BLACK DIAGONAL PRINT:**
- Cut 3, 2-3/4 x 42-inch strips

Sew the binding to the quilt using a 3/8-inch seam allowance. This measurement will produce a 1/2-inch wide finished double binding. Refer to *Binding* and *Diagonal Piecing* on page 159 for complete instructions.

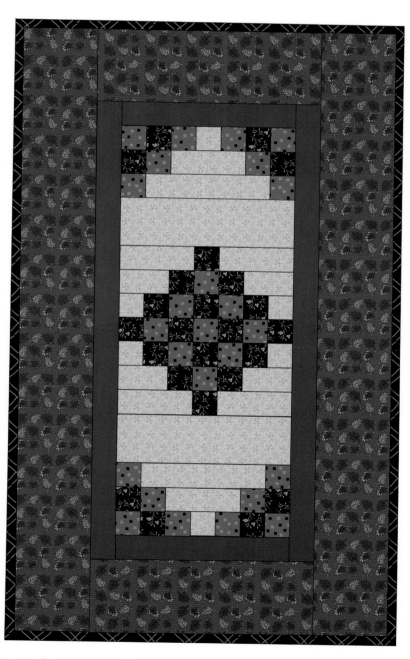

Mini Cherry Berry — Autumn Runner

15 x 25-inches

Fresh as a spring breeze, this quilt covers the table with a gentle hint of sunshine in the center surrounded by a sawtooth border. The vintage yardsticks framed as art are premiums offered by local businesses and collected from hardware stores.

Spring Breeze

Tablecloth

70-inches square

Fabrics and Supplies

1 yard **CREAM PRINT** for center block

1 yard **RED PRINT**
for sawtooth border and middle border

3/8 yard **LIGHT GOLD PRINT**
for sawtooth border

3/8 yard **GREEN PRINT**
for corner squares and narrow inner border

3/8 yard **MEDIUM GOLD PRINT**
for wide inner border

2-1/8 yards **GREEN FLORAL**
for corner squares and outer border

2/3 yard **GREEN PRINT** for binding

4-1/4 yards of 42-inch wide fabric for backing
or
2-1/8 yards of 108-inch wide fabric
for backing

quilt batting, at least 76-inches square

Quilt Center

Cutting

From **CREAM PRINT:**
- Cut 1, 32-1/2-inch center square

From **RED PRINT:**
- Cut 2, 4-7/8 x 42-inch strips

From **LIGHT GOLD PRINT:**
- Cut 2, 4-7/8 x 42-inch strips

From **GREEN PRINT:**
- Cut 1, 4-1/2 x 42-inch strip. From the strip cut: 4, 4-1/2-inch corner squares

Piecing

Step 1 With right sides together, layer the 4-7/8 x 42-inch **RED** and **LIGHT GOLD** strips in pairs. Press together, but do not sew. Cut the layered strips into squares. Cut the layered squares in half diagonally to make 32 sets of triangles. Stitch 1/4-inch from the diagonal edge of each pair of triangles; press.

Crosscut 16, 4-7/8-inch squares

Make 32, 4-1/2-inch triangle-pieced squares

Step 2 For each of the sawtooth borders, sew 8 of the Step 1 triangle-pieced squares together; press. <u>At this point each sawtooth border should measure 4-1/2 x 32-1/2-inches.</u> Sew 2 of the sawtooth borders to the top/bottom edges of the 32-1/2-inch **CREAM** square; press.

Make 4

Step 3 Sew the 4-1/2-inch **GREEN** corner squares to both ends of the remaining sawtooth borders; press. Sew the sawtooth borders to the side edges of the Step 2 unit; press. <u>At this point the table square center should measure 40-1/2-inches square.</u>

Borders

*Note: The yardage given allows for the border strips to be cut on the crosswise grain. Diagonally piece the strips as needed, referring to **Diagonal Piecing** instructions on page 159. Read through **Border** instructions on page 158 for general instructions on adding borders.*

Cutting

From MEDIUM GOLD PRINT:
- Cut 4, 2-1/2 x 42-inch wide inner border strips

From GREEN PRINT:
- Cut 4, 1-1/2 x 42-inch narrow inner border strips

From RED PRINT:
- Cut 6, 3-1/2 x 42-inch middle border strips

From GREEN FLORAL:
- Cut 7, 9-1/2 x 42-inch outer border strips
- Cut 1, 3-1/2 x 42-inch strip. From the strip cut: 4, 3-1/2-inch corner squares

Attaching the Borders

Step 1 Aligning long edges, sew the 2-1/2 x 42-inch **MEDIUM GOLD** strips and the 1-1/2 x 42-inch **GREEN** strips together in pairs; press. Make 4 pieced border strips. To attach the top/bottom border strips, refer to page 158 for complete *Border* instructions.

Step 2 For the side borders, measure the tablecloth from top to bottom, including the seam allowances but not the borders just added. Cut the 3-1/2-inch wide pieced border strips to this length. Sew 3-1/2-inch **GREEN FLORAL** corner squares to both ends of the pieced border strips; press. Sew the border strips to the side edges of the tablecloth center; press.

Step 3 Attach the 3-1/2-inch wide **RED** middle border strips.

Step 4 Attach the 9-1/2-inch wide **GREEN FLORAL** outer border strips.

Putting It All Together

Cut the 4-1/4 yard length of backing fabric in half crosswise to make 2, 2-1/8 yard lengths. Refer to **Finishing the Quilt** on page 159 for complete instructions.

Quilting Suggestions:

- Cream center block - 4-inch grid.
- Red sawtooth - echo quilt.
- Light Gold sawtooth - meander.
- Green corner squares - TB23 Floral Burst (2 inner flowers only).
- Medium Gold, Green, and Red borders - quilt as one with TB37 Pansy Vine.
- Green Floral outer border - large meander.

*The **THIMBLEBERRIES**® quilt stencils are by Quilting Creations International.*

Binding

Cutting

From GREEN PRINT:
- Cut 8, 2-3/4 x 42-inch strips

Sew the binding to the quilt using a 3/8-inch seam allowance. This measurement will produce a 1/2-inch wide finished double binding. Refer to **Binding** and **Diagonal Piecing** on page 159 for complete instructions.

TB23 Floral Burst Quilting Suggestion

TB37 Pansy Vine Quilting Suggestion

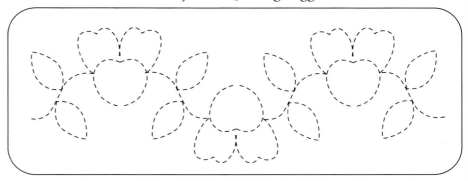

Spring Breeze Tablecloth

70-inches square

Autumn's first frost brings out the best in sugar maples. Leaves turn from bright green to golden brown and deeper shades of rust as the season slowly gives way to winter's snowflakes.

Sugar Maples

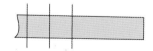

Throw

60 x 72-inches

Fabrics and Supplies

7/8 yard **GREEN PRINT**
for leaf blocks and lattice post squares

1 yard **BEIGE PRINT** for leaf blocks,
nine-patch blocks, and pieced border

1-7/8 yards **TAN/RED FLORAL** for
nine-patch blocks and outer border

3/4 yard **GOLD PRINT**
for lattice and inner border

5/8 yard **DARK BROWN PRINT**
for pieced border

1/3 yard **RED FLORAL** for pieced border

1/2 yard **RED DIAGONAL PRINT**
for middle border

3/8 yard **MEDIUM BROWN PRINT**
for narrow middle border

3/4 yard **DARK BROWN PRINT**
for binding

3-3/4 yards for backing

quilt batting, at least 66 x 78-inches

Leaf Blocks

Makes 16 blocks

Cutting

From **GREEN PRINT:**

- Cut 2, 4-1/2 x 42-inch strips. From the strips cut:
  16, 4-1/2-inch squares
- Cut 3, 2-7/8 x 42-inch strips
- Cut 1, 2-1/2 x 42-inch strip. From the strip cut:
  16, 2-1/2-inch squares

From **BEIGE PRINT:**

- Cut 3, 2-7/8 x 42-inch strips

Piecing

Step 1 With right sides together, layer the
2-7/8 x 42-inch **GREEN** and **BEIGE** strips in
pairs. Press together, but do not sew. Cut the
layered strips into squares. Cut the layered
squares in half diagonally to make 64 sets of
triangles. Stitch 1/4-inch from the diagonal edge
of each pair of triangles; press.

Crosscut 32, 2-7/8-inch squares

Make 64, 2-1/2-inch triangle-pieced squares

Step 2 Referring to the diagrams, sew the triangle-pieced squares together in pairs to make A Units and B Units; press. Sew a 2-1/2-inch **GREEN** square to the left edge of each B Unit; press. Referring to the leaf block diagram, sew 1 of the A Units to the top edge of each 4-1/2-inch **GREEN** square; press. Sew 1 of the B Units to the right edge of each square; press. <u>At this point each leaf block should measure 6-1/2-inches square.</u>

Unit A
Make 16

Unit B
Make 16

Make 16

Nine-Patch Blocks

Makes 14 blocks

Cutting

From **BEIGE PRINT:**
- Cut 4, 2-1/2 x 42-inch strips

From **TAN/RED FLORAL:**
- Cut 5, 2-1/2 x 42-inch strips

Piecing

Step 1 Aligning long edges, sew 2-1/2 x 42-inch **TAN/RED FLORAL** strips to both sides of a 2-1/2 x 42-inch **BEIGE** strip. Press the seam allowances toward the **TAN/RED FLORAL** fabric, referring to *Hints and Helps for Pressing Strip Sets* on page 158. Make a total of 2 strip sets; cut into segments.

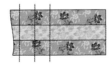

Crosscut 28, 2-1/2-inch wide segments

Step 2 Aligning long edges, sew 2-1/2 x 42-inch **BEIGE** strips to both sides of a 2-1/2 x 42-inch **TAN/RED FLORAL** strip; press and cut into segments.

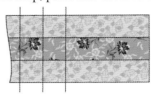

Crosscut 14, 2-1/2-inch wide segments

Step 3 Sew Step 1 units to both side edges of a Step 2 unit; press. <u>At this point each nine-patch block should measure 6-1/2-inches square.</u>

Make 14

Quilt Center

Cutting

From **GOLD PRINT:**
- Cut 4, 2-1/2 x 42-inch strips. From the strips cut: 12, 2-1/2 x 12-1/2-inch lattice segments

From **GREEN PRINT:**
- Cut 1, 2-1/2 x 42-inch strip. From the strip cut: 9, 2-1/2-inch lattice post squares

Quilt Center Assembly

Step 1 Referring to the diagram for placement, sew 8 of the leaf blocks and 8 of the nine-patch blocks together in pairs; press. Make 8 pairs. Sew the pairs together; press. <u>At this point each unit should measure 12-1/2-inches square.</u>

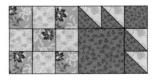

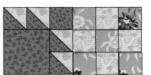

Make 4

Step 2 Referring to the quilt diagram, sew together 2 of the Step 1 units and 3 of the 2-1/2 x 12-1/2-inch **GOLD** lattice segments. Press the seam allowances toward the **GOLD** strips. Make 2 block rows.

Step 3 Sew together 2 of the 2-1/2 x 12-1/2-inch **GOLD** lattice segments and 3 of the 2-1/2-inch **GREEN** lattice post squares. Press the seam allowances toward the **GOLD** strips. Make 3 lattice strips.

Step 4 Sew the block rows and lattice strips together; press. At this point the quilt center should measure 30-1/2-inches square.

Pieced Border

Cutting

From **DARK BROWN PRINT**:

- Cut 7, 2-1/2 x 42-inch strips. From the strips cut:
20, 2-1/2 x 6-1/2-inch rectangles
48, 2-1/2-inch squares

From **BEIGE PRINT**:

- Cut 4, 2-1/2 x 42-inch strips. From the strips cut:
20, 2-1/2 x 6-1/2-inch rectangles

From **RED FLORAL**:

- Cut 3, 2-1/2 x 42-inch strips. From the strips cut:
48, 2-1/2-inch squares

Piecing

Step 1 With right sides together, position 2-1/2-inch **DARK BROWN** squares on the corners of a 2-1/2 x 6-1/2-inch **BEIGE** rectangle. Draw a diagonal line on the squares and stitch on the line. Trim the seam allowances to 1/4-inch; press. Referring to the diagram sew 5 units together; press. Make 4 pieced border strips. At this point each pieced border strip should measure 2-1/2 x 30-1/2-inches.

Make 20

Make 4

Step 2 With right sides together, position 2-1/2-inch **RED FLORAL** squares on the corners of a 2-1/2 x 6-1/2-inch **DARK BROWN** rectangle. Draw a diagonal line on the squares; stitch, trim, and press. Referring to the diagram sew 5 units together; press. Make 4 pieced border strips. At this point each pieced border strip should measure 2-1/2 x 30-1/2-inches.

Make 20

Make 4

Step 3 Sew the Step 2 pieced borders to the top edge of the Step 1 pieced borders; press. Make 4 pieced borders. At this point each pieced border strip should measure 4-1/2 x 30-1/2-inches. Sew 2 of the pieced borders to the top/bottom edges of the quilt center; press.

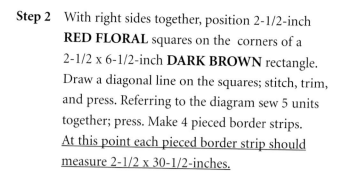

Make 4

Step 4 Sew together the 2-1/2-inch **RED FLORAL** and **DARK BROWN** squares in pairs; press. Sew together the pairs to make four-patch blocks; press. Sew the four-patch blocks to the ends of the remaining Step 3 pieced borders. Sew the pieced borders to the side edges of the quilt center; press. At this point the quilt center should measure 38-1/2-inches square.

Make 8

Make 4

Quilt Assembly and Borders

*Note: The yardage given allows for the border strips to be cut on the crosswise grain. Diagonally piece the strips as needed, referring to **Diagonal Piecing** instructions on page 159. Read through **Border** instructions on page 158 for general instructions on adding borders.*

Cutting

From **GOLD PRINT**:
- Cut 5, 2-1/2 x 42-inch inner border strips

From **RED DIAGONAL PRINT**:
- Cut 6, 2-1/2 x 42-inch middle border strips

From **MEDIUM BROWN PRINT**:
- Cut 6, 1-1/2 x 42-inch narrow middle border strips

From **TAN/RED FLORAL**:
- Cut 7, 6-1/2 x 42-inch outer border strips

Attaching the Borders

Step 1   Attach the 2-1/2-inch wide **GOLD** inner border strips.

Step 2   Sew together 4 of the leaf blocks and 3 of the nine-patch blocks; press. Make 2 strips and sew them to the top/bottom edges of the quilt center; press.

Step 3   Attach the 2-1/2-inch wide **RED DIAGONAL PRINT** middle border strips.

Step 4   Attach the 1-1/2-inch wide **MEDIUM BROWN** narrow middle border strips.

Step 5   Attach the 6-1/2-inch wide **TAN/RED FLORAL** outer border strips.

Putting It All Together

Cut the 3-3/4 yard length of backing fabric in half crosswise to make 2, 1-7/8 yard lengths. Refer to *Finishing the Quilt* on page 159 for complete instructions.

Binding

Cutting

From **DARK BROWN PRINT**:
- Cut 7, 2-3/4 x 42-inch strips

Sew the binding to the quilt using a 3/8-inch seam allowance. This measurement will produce a 1/2-inch wide finished double binding. Refer to **Binding** and **Diagonal Piecing** on page 159 for complete instructions.

Sugar Maples Throw
60 x 72-inches

The center square for each of the blocks is fussy cut to showcase the large rose floral fabric reminiscent of an old-fashioned spring garden in full bloom.

Spring Garland

Quilt

71-1/2 x 92-1/2-inches

Fabrics and Supplies

4 yds **LARGE ROSE FLORAL** for center squares (we fussy cut our squares), middle border, and outer border

1-2/3 yards **BEIGE PRINT** for pieced blocks

1-5/8 yards **BLUE PRINT** for pieced blocks and lattice posts

1 yard **RED PRINT** for lattice segments

1 yard **GREEN PRINT** for inner and middle borders

1 yard **RED CHECK** for binding (cut on the bias)

5-1/2 yards for backing

quilt batting, at least 78 x 99-inches

Pieced Blocks

Makes 24 blocks

Cutting

From **LARGE ROSE FLORAL:**
- Cut 24, 3-1/2-inch center squares (we fussy cut our squares)

From **BEIGE PRINT:**
- Cut 4, 3 x 42-inch strips. From the strips cut: 48, 3-inch squares. Cut the squares in half diagonally to make 96 triangles.
- Cut 10, 2-3/8 x 42-inch strips
- Cut 9, 2 x 42-inch strips. From the strips cut: 96, 2 x 3-1/2-inch rectangles

From **BLUE PRINT:**
- Cut 5, 3-7/8 x 42-inch strips. From the strips cut: 48, 3-7/8-inch squares. Cut the squares in half diagonally to make 96 triangles.
- Cut 10, 2-3/8 x 42-inch strips

Piecing

Step 1 With right sides together, position a **BEIGE** triangle on the top edge of a 3-1/2-inch **LARGE ROSE FLORAL** square. Stitch with a 1/4-inch seam allowance. Repeat this process for the bottom edge of the square; press. Sew **BEIGE** triangles to the side edges of the square; press. <u>At this point each square should measure 4-3/4-inches.</u>

Make 24

Step 2 With right sides together, position a **BLUE** triangle on the side edge of a Step 1 square; stitch. Repeat this process for the opposite side edge of the square; press. Sew **BLUE** triangles to the 2 remaining side edges of the square; press. At this point each square should measure 6-1/2-inches square.

Make 24

Step 3 With right sides together, layer the 2-3/8 x 42-inch **BLUE** and **BEIGE** strips in pairs. Press together, but do not sew. Cut the layered strips into squares. Cut the layered squares in half diagonally to make 288 sets of triangles. Stitch 1/4-inch from the diagonal edge of each pair of triangles; press.

Crosscut 144, 2-3/8-inch squares

Make 288, 2-inch triangle-pieced squares

Step 4 Sew Step 3 triangle-pieced squares to both side edges of the 2 x 3-1/2-inch **BEIGE** rectangles; press. At this point each unit should measure 2 x 6-1/2-inches.

Make 96 units

Step 5 Sew 2 of the Step 4 units to the side edges of the Step 2 center squares; press.

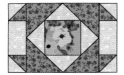

Make 24

Step 6 Sew Step 3 triangle-pieced squares to the top/bottom edges of the remaining Step 4 units; press. At this point each unit should measure 2 x 9-1/2-inches.

Make 48

Step 7 Sew the Step 6 units to the side edges of the center squares to make a pieced block; press. At this point each pieced block should measure 9-1/2-inches square.

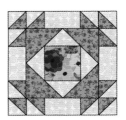

Make 24

Quilt Center

Cutting

From RED PRINT:

- Cut 15, 2 x 42-inch strips. From the strips cut: 58, 2 x 9-1/2-inch lattice segments

From BLUE PRINT:

- Cut 2, 2 x 42-inch strips. From the strips cut: 35, 2-inch lattice post squares

Quilt Center Assembly

Step 1 Sew together 4 of the pieced blocks and 5 of the 2 x 9-1/2-inch **RED** lattice segments. Press the seam allowances toward the lattice segments. At this point each block row should measure 9-1/2 x 44-inches.

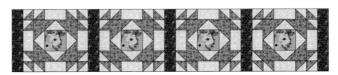

Make 6

Step 2 Sew together 5 of the 2-inch **BLUE** lattice post squares and 4 of the 2 x 9-1/2-inch **RED** lattice segments. Press the seam allowances toward the lattice segments. <u>At this point each lattice strip should measure 2 x 44-inches.</u>

Make 7

Step 3 Sew the block rows and lattice strips together; press. <u>At this point the quilt center should measure 44 x 65-inches.</u>

Borders

*Note: The yardage given allows for the border strips to be cut on the crosswise grain. Diagonally piece the strips as needed, referring to **Diagonal Piecing** instructions on page 159. Read through **Border** instructions on page 158 for general instructions on adding borders.*

Cutting

From **GREEN PRINT:**
- Cut 14, 2 x 42-inch inner and narrow middle border strips

From **LARGE ROSE FLORAL:**
- Cut 10, 9 x 42-inch outer border strips
- Cut 7, 3 x 42-inch wide middle border strips

Attaching the Borders

Step 1 Attach the 2-inch wide **GREEN** inner border strips.

Step 2 Attach the 3-inch wide **LARGE ROSE FLORAL** wide middle border strips.

Step 3 Attach the 2-inch wide **GREEN** narrow middle border strips.

Step 4 Attach the 9-inch wide **LARGE ROSE FLORAL** outer border strips.

Putting It All Together

Cut the 5-1/2 yard length of backing fabric in half crosswise to make 2, 2-3/4 yard lengths. Refer to ***Finishing the Quilt*** on page 159 for complete instructions.

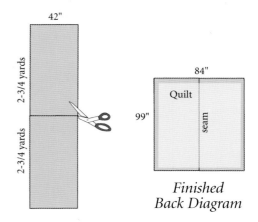

Finished Back Diagram

Binding

Cutting

From **RED CHECK:**
- Cut enough 2-3/4-inch wide **bias** strips to make a 340-inch long strip.

Sew the binding to the quilt using a 3/8-inch seam allowance. This measurement will produce a 1/2-inch wide finished double binding. Refer to ***Binding*** and ***Diagonal Piecing*** on page 159 for complete instructions.

Irresistible children's chairs with well-worn spindles and chipped paint are favorite flea market finds waiting to be welcomed into a home filled with other reminders of years gone by. The palette of the pieced blocks and lattice posts in the Spring Garland quilt complement the display.

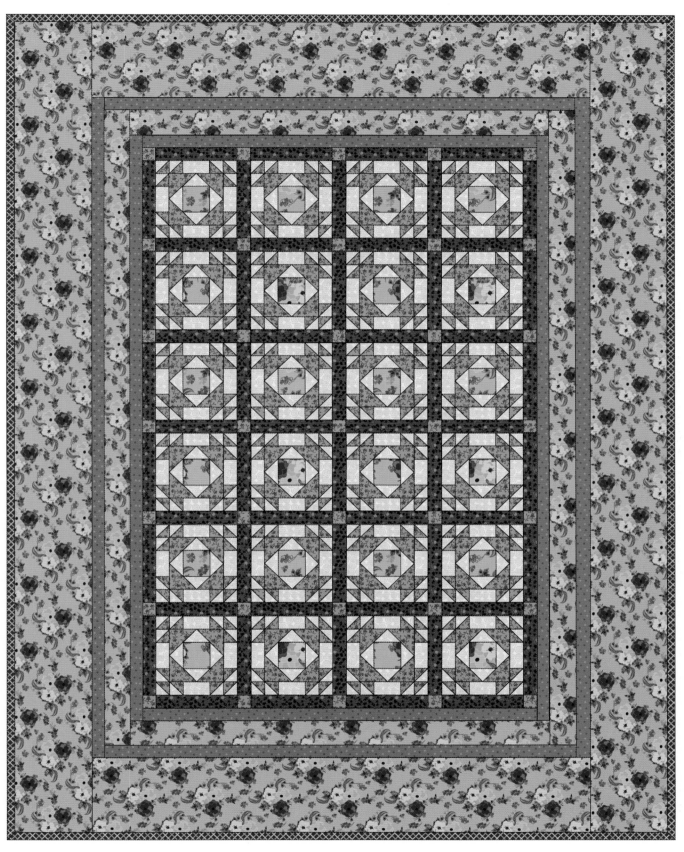

Spring Garland Quilt

71-1/2 x 92-1/2-inches

Patchwork and embroidery go hand in hand when embroidery floss colors complement fabric choices. A little brown bird on a branch in bloom adds old-fashioned charm to a ruffled patchwork pillow.

Little Brown Bird

Pillow

18-inches square

Fabrics and Supplies

1/3 yard **BEIGE PRINT #1** for center square

1/8 yard **ROSE PRINT** for inner border

1/8 yard **BEIGE PRINT #2** for checkerboard

5/8 yard **GREEN PRINT**
for checkerboard and outer ruffle

1-1/3 yards **LARGE ROSE FLORAL** for
outer border, inner ruffle, and pillow back

embroidery floss for decorative stitches:
gold, dark green, light green, red, blue,
dark gold, medium brown, dark brown

5/8 yard muslin backing for pillow top

quilt batting, at least 20-inches square

18-inch square pillow form

Center Square

Cutting

From **BEIGE PRINT #1:**

- Cut 1, 11-inch square. The square will be trimmed to 8-1/2-inches when the embroidery is complete.

Embroidering the Center Square

Step 1 Transfer the embroidery design on page 72 onto the 11-inch **BEIGE #1** center square by positioning the square over the tracing diagram. Lightly trace the embroidery design onto the fabric.

Step 2 With 3 strands of embroidery floss, stitch the design with the outline stitch, straight stitch, lazy daisy, and French knot.

Straight stitch

French knot

Lazy daisy stitch

Outline/stem stitch

Step 3 Trim the embroidered square to 8-1/2-inches.

Borders

Note: *The yardage given allows for the border strips to be cut on the crosswise grain. Read through* **Border** *instructions on page 158 for general instructions on adding borders.*

Cutting

From **ROSE PRINT:**
- Cut 1, 2 x 42-inch strip. From the strip cut:
  2, 2 x 8-1/2-inch strips
  2, 2 x 11-1/2-inch strips

From **BEIGE PRINT #2:**
- Cut 1, 1-1/2 x 42-inch strip for checkerboard

From **GREEN PRINT:**
- Cut 1, 1-1/2 x 42-inch strip for checkerboard

From **LARGE ROSE FLORAL:**
- Cut 2, 3 x 42-inch outer border strips

Attaching the Borders

Step 1 Sew the 2 x 8-1/2-inch **ROSE** strips to the top/bottom edges of the embroidered center square; press. Sew the 2 x 11-1/2-inch **ROSE** strips to the side edges of the center square; press.

Step 2 Aligning long edges, sew together the 1-1/2 x 42-inch **BEIGE #2** and **GREEN** strips; press. Cut the strip set into segments.

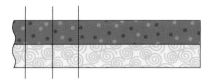

Crosscut 26, 1-1/2-inch wide segments

Step 3 Sew 6 segments together for the top/bottom checkerboard borders; press. Remove a **BEIGE #2** square from 1 end of each strip. Sew the borders to the top/bottom edges of the pillow top; press.

Make 2

Step 4 Sew 7 segments together for the side checkerboard borders; press. Remove a **GREEN** square from 1 end of each strip. Sew the borders to the side edges of the pillow top; press.

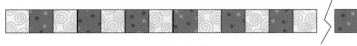

Make 2

Step 5 Attach the 3-inch wide **LARGE ROSE FLORAL** outer border strips.

Putting It All Together

Step 1 Trim the muslin pillow top backing and batting so they are 2-inches larger than the pillow top dimensions.

Step 2 Layer the muslin backing, batting, and pillow top. Baste the layers together; quilt as desired. The outer border was quilted with THIMBLEBERRIES® quilt stencil TB27 Heart Vine Border by Quilting Creations International.

Step 3 When quilting is complete, trim the excess backing and batting even with the pillow top.

Note: *To prepare the pillow top before attaching the ruffle, I suggest hand basting the edges of all 3 layers of the pillow top together. This will prevent the edge of the pillow top from rippling when you attach the ruffle.*

Pillow Ruffle

Note: *By sewing 2 different width fabrics together, you form the illusion of a double ruffle without additional bulk.*

Cutting

From **LARGE ROSE FLORAL:**
- Cut 5, 2-5/8 x 42-inch strips for the inner ruffle

From **GREEN PRINT:**
- Cut 5, 3-5/8 x 42-inch strips for the outer ruffle

Piecing and Attaching the Ruffle

Step 1 Diagonally piece the 2-5/8-inch wide **LARGE ROSE FLORAL** strips together, referring to *Diagonal Piecing* instructions on page 159.

Step 2 Diagonally piece the 3-5/8-inch wide **GREEN** strips together.

Step 3 Aligning long raw edges, sew the **LARGE ROSE FLORAL** strip and the **GREEN** strip together; press. With right sides facing, sew the short raw edges together with a diagonal seam to make a continuous circle. Trim the seam allowance to 1/4-inch; press.

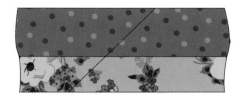

Step 4 Fold the strip in half lengthwise, wrong sides together; press. Divide the ruffle strip into 4 equal segments; mark the quarter points with safety pins.

Step 5 To gather the ruffle, position a heavyweight thread 1/4-inch from the raw edge of the folded ruffle strip. You will need a length of thread 144-inches long. Secure 1 end of the heavy thread by stitching across it. Then zigzag stitch over the thread all the way around the ruffle strip, taking care not to sew through the thread.

Secure   Zigzag

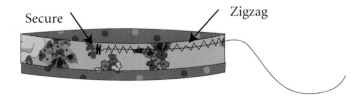

Step 6 With right sides together, pin the ruffle to the pillow top, matching the quarter points of the ruffle to the corners of the pillow. Pin in place.

Step 7 Gently pull the gathering stitches until the ruffle fits the pillow top; taking care to allow a little extra

ruffle at each corner for a full look. Pin in place and machine baste the ruffle to the pillow top, using a 1/4-inch seam allowance.

Pillow Back

Cutting

From LARGE ROSE FLORAL:
- Cut 1, 26 x 42-inch strip. From the strip cut: 2, 18-1/2 x 26-inch rectangles

Assemble the Pillow Back

Step 1 With wrong sides together, fold the 2, 18-1/2 x 26-inch rectangles in half to form 2, 13 x 18-1/2-inch double-thick pillow back pieces.

Step 2 Overlap the 2 folded edges so that the pillow back measures 18-1/2-inches square; pin. Stitch around the entire pillow back to create a single pillow back. The double thickness of each back piece will make the pillow back more stable and give it a nice finishing touch.

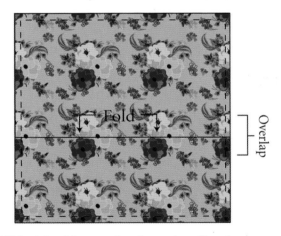

Step 3 With right sides together, layer the pillow back and the pillow top; pin. The ruffle will be sandwiched between the 2 layers and turned in toward the center of the pillow at this time. Stitch around the outside edge, using a 3/8-inch seam allowance.

Step 4 Turn the pillow right side out and fluff up the ruffle. Insert the pillow form through the back opening.

Embroidery Design

Little Brown Bird Pillow
18-inches square

*Flea market toys pair up with big,
bold quilt blocks for a
family-friendly addition to any room.*

Square-in-a-Square

Throw

74 x 90-inches

Fabrics and Supplies

4-1/4 yards **BLUE DOT**
for square-in-a-square blocks, inner border, dogtooth border, and outer border

2-3/4 yards **YELLOW PRINT**
for square-in-a-square blocks, alternate blocks, quilt center, and dogtooth border

1-3/4 yards **RED PRINT** for hourglass blocks and corner squares

1-1/2 yards **BEIGE PRINT** for hourglass blocks and quilt center

2 yards **RED CHECK PLAID** for binding (cut on the bias)

5-1/3 yards for backing

quilt batting, at least 80 x 96-inches

Square-in-a-Square Blocks

Makes 12 blocks

Cutting

From **BLUE DOT**:
- Cut 3, 8-1/2 x 42-inch strips. From the strips cut: 12, 8-1/2-inch squares

From **YELLOW PRINT**:
- Cut 6, 4-1/2 x 42-inch strips. From the strips cut: 48, 4-1/2-inch squares

Piecing

With right sides together, position 4-1/2-inch **YELLOW** squares on 2 opposite corners of an 8-1/2-inch **BLUE DOT** square. Draw diagonal lines on the squares and stitch on the lines. Trim the seam allowances to 1/4-inch; press the seam allowances toward the **YELLOW** triangles. Repeat this process at the 2 remaining corners of the **BLUE DOT** square. <u>At this point each square-in-a-square block should measure 8-1/2-inches square.</u>

Make 12

Hourglass Blocks

Makes 17 blocks

Cutting

From **RED PRINT**:
- Cut 3, 9-1/4 x 42-inch strips

From **BEIGE PRINT**:
- Cut 3, 9-1/4 x 42-inch strips

Piecing

Step 1 With right sides together, layer the 9-1/4 x 42-inch **RED** and **BEIGE** strips in pairs; press. From the layered strips cut: 9, 9-1/4-inch squares. Cut the squares diagonally into quarters to make 36 triangle sets. You will be using only 34 triangle sets.

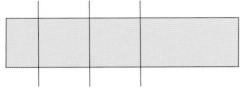

Crosscut 9, 9-1/4-inch squares

Step 2 Stitch along 1 bias edge of a triangle set; press. Repeat this process with the remaining **RED** and **BEIGE** triangle sets, stitching along the same bias edge of each set to make a triangle unit. Sew the triangle units together in pairs; press. <u>At this point each hourglass block should measure 8-1/2-inches square.</u>

Bias edges

Make 34   *Make 17*

Quilt Center

Cutting

From RED PRINT:
- Cut 4, 4-1/2 x 42-inch strips. From the strips cut: 14, 4-1/2 x 8-1/2-inch rectangles
- Cut 4, 4-1/2-inch corner squares (set aside)

From BEIGE PRINT:
- Cut 4, 4-1/2 x 42-inch strips. From the strips cut: 28, 4-1/2-inch squares

From YELLOW PRINT:
- Cut 2, 8-1/2 x 42-inch strips. From the strips cut: 6, 8-1/2-inch alternate block squares
- Cut 3, 4-1/2 x 42-inch strips. From the strips cut: 10, 4-1/2 x 8-1/2-inch rectangles 4, 4-1/2-inch corner squares

Quilt Center Assembly

Step 1 With right sides together, position a 4-1/2-inch **BEIGE** square on the corner of a 4-1/2 x 8-1/2-inch **RED** rectangle. Draw a diagonal line on the square; stitch and trim. Press the seam allowances toward the lighter fabric. Repeat this process at the opposite corner of the rectangle.

Make 14

Step 2 To make the top/bottom quilt center strips, sew together 3 of the Step 1 units, 2 of the 4-1/2 x 8-1/2-inch **YELLOW** rectangles, and 2 of the 4-1/2-inch **YELLOW** corner squares. Press the seam allowances toward the **YELLOW** fabric. <u>At this point each strip should measure 4-1/2 x 48-1/2-inches.</u>

Make 2

Step 3 To make the square-in-a-square/hourglass block rows, sew together 3 of the square-in-a-square blocks, 2 of the hourglass blocks, and 2 of the Step 1 units. Press the seam allowances toward the square-in-a-square blocks. <u>At this point each block row should measure 8-1/2 x 48-1/2-inches.</u>

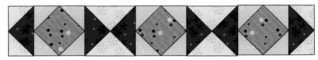

Make 4

Step 4 To make the hourglass/alternate block rows, sew together 3 of the hourglass blocks, 2 of the 8-1/2-inch **YELLOW** alternate block squares, and 2 of the 4-1/2 x 8-1/2-inch **YELLOW** rectangles. Press the seam allowances toward the alternate blocks. <u>At this point each block row should measure 8-1/2 x 48-1/2-inches.</u>

Make 3

Step 5 Referring to the quilt assembly diagram, lay out the block rows from Steps 2, 3, and 4. Pin them together at the block intersections; sew together. Press the seam allowances in 1 direction. At this point the quilt center should measure 48-1/2 x 64-1/2-inches.

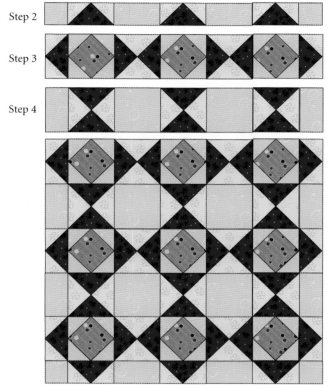

Quilt Assembly Diagram

Borders

*Note: The yardage given allows for the border strips to be cut on the crosswise grain. Diagonally piece the strips as needed, referring to **Diagonal Piecing** instructions on page 159. Read through **Border** instructions on page 158 for general instructions on adding borders.*

Cutting

From **BLUE DOT**:
- Cut 9, 5-1/2 x 42-inch outer border strips
- Cut 7, 4-1/2 x 42-inch inner border strips
- Cut 8, 4-1/2 x 42-inch strips. From the strips cut: 64, 4-1/2-inch squares

From **YELLOW PRINT**:
- Cut 8, 4-1/2 x 42-inch strips. From the strips cut: 32, 4-1/2 x 8-1/2-inch rectangles

The 4, 4-1/2-inch **RED PRINT** corner squares were cut previously.

Assembling and Attaching the Borders

Step 1 Attach the 4-1/2-inch wide **BLUE DOT** inner border strips.

Step 2 With right sides together, position a 4-1/2-inch **BLUE DOT** square on the corner of a 4-1/2 x 8-1/2-inch **YELLOW** rectangle. Draw a diagonal line on the square; stitch, trim, and press. Repeat this process at the opposite corner of the rectangle.

Make 32

Step 3 To make the top/bottom dogtooth borders, sew together 7 of the Step 2 units; press. At this point each dogtooth border strip should measure 4-1/2 x 56-1/2-inches. Sew the pieced borders to the quilt center; press the seam allowances toward the inner border.

Step 4 To make the side dogtooth borders, sew together 9 of the Step 2 units; press. Sew 4-1/2-inch **RED** corner squares to both ends of the border strips; press. At this point each dogtooth border strip should measure 4-1/2 x 72-1/2-inches. Sew the dogtooth borders to the quilt center; press.

Step 5 Attach the 5-1/2-inch wide **BLUE DOT** outer border strips.

Putting It All Together

Cut the 5-1/3 yard length of backing fabric in half crosswise to make 2, 2-2/3 yard lengths. Refer to *Finishing the Quilt* on page 159 for complete instructions.

Binding

Cutting

From RED PLAID CHECK:

- Cut enough 6-1/2-inch wide **bias** strips to make a 340-inch long strip.

Sew the binding to the quilt using a scant 1-inch seam allowance. This measurement will produce a 1-inch wide finished double binding. Refer to ***Binding*** and ***Diagonal Piecing*** instructions on page 159 for complete instructions.

"And to all a goodnight" is a thread that runs through Jan's family as well as mine. When the grandchildren come to visit, a welcoming quilt offers soft comfort to kids of any age. Here, Clayton and Hank cuddle up to comfort in the Square-in-a-Square Throw.

Square-in-a-Square Throw
74 x 90-inches

Patches of sunlight peek through the
spinning blades of this dramatic
combination of contrasting light and dark fabrics.

Sunshine Patches

Throw

80 x 96-inches

Fabrics and Supplies

1-5/8 yards **ROSE PRINT** for blocks

2-2/3 yards **GREEN PRINT** for blocks and flying geese border

7/8 yard **GOLD PLAID** for blocks

4-7/8 yards **BLUE PRINT** for blocks, and inner and outer borders

2 yards **BEIGE PRINT** for blocks and flying geese border

1 yard **GOLD PLAID** for binding (cut on the bias)

7-1/8 yards for backing

quilt batting, at least 86 x 102-inches

Pieced Blocks

Makes 12 blocks

Cutting

From **ROSE PRINT**:
- Cut 12, 4-1/2 x 42-inch strips. From the strips cut: 96, 4-1/2-inch squares

From **GREEN PRINT**:
- Cut 12, 4-1/2 x 42-inch strips. From the strips cut: 48, 4-1/2 x 8-1/2-inch rectangles

From **GOLD PLAID**:
- Cut 6, 4-1/2 x 42-inch strips. From the strips cut: 48, 4-1/2-inch squares

From **BLUE PRINT**:
- Cut 12, 4-1/2 x 42-inch strips. From the strips cut: 48, 4-1/2 x 8-1/2-inch rectangles

From **BEIGE PRINT**:
- Cut 6, 4-1/2 x 42-inch strips. From the strips cut: 48, 4-1/2-inch squares

Piecing

Step 1 With right sides together, position a 4-1/2-inch **GOLD PLAID** square on the left corner of a 4-1/2 x 8-1/2-inch **GREEN** rectangle. Draw a diagonal line on the square and stitch on the line. Trim the seam allowance to 1/4-inch; press. Repeat this process at the opposite corner of the rectangle using a 4-1/2-inch **ROSE** square.

Make 28

Step 2 With right sides together, position a 4-1/2-inch **ROSE** square on the left corner of a 4-1/2 x 8-1/2-inch **BLUE** rectangle. Draw a diagonal line on the square; stitch, trim, and press. Repeat this process at the opposite corner of the rectangle using a 4-1/2-inch **BEIGE** square.

Make 48

Step 3 Sew the Step 1 and Step 2 units together in pairs; press. <u>At this point each unit should measure 8-1/2-inches square.</u>

Make 48

Step 4 Sew the Step 3 units together in pairs; press. Sew the pairs together to make the pieced block. <u>At this point each pieced block should measure 16-1/2-inches square.</u>

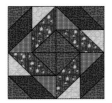

Make 12

Step 5 Referring to the quilt diagram for block placement, sew the blocks together in 4 rows of 3 blocks each. Press the seam allowances in alternating directions by rows so the seams fit snugly together with less bulk. <u>At this point each block row should measure 16-1/2 x 48-1/2-inches.</u>

Step 6 Pin the block rows together at the block intersections. Sew the rows together to make the quilt center; press. <u>At this point the quilt center should measure 48-1/2 x 64-1/2-inches.</u>

Borders

Note: *The yardage given allows for the border strips to be cut on the crosswise grain. Diagonally piece the*

strips as needed, referring to **Diagonal Piecing** *instructions on page 159. Read through* **Border** *instructions on page 158 for general instructions on adding borders.*

Cutting

From **BLUE PRINT**:
- Cut 10, 8-1/2 x 42-inch outer border strips
- Cut 7, 4-1/2 x 42-inch inner border strips

From **GREEN PRINT:**
- Cut 8, 4-1/2 x 42-inch strips. From the strips cut: 32, 4-1/2 x 8-1/2-inch rectangles 4, 4-1/2-inch corner squares

From **BEIGE PRINT**:
- Cut 8, 4-1/2 x 42-inch strips. From the strips cut: 64, 4-1/2-inch squares

Assembling and Attaching the Borders

Step 1 Attach the 4-1/2-inch wide **BLUE** inner borders.

Step 2 With right sides together, position a 4-1/2-inch **BEIGE** square on the corner of a 4-1/2 x 8-1/2-inch **GREEN** rectangle. Draw a diagonal line on the square; stitch, trim, and press. Repeat this process at the opposite corner of the rectangle.

Make 32 flying geese units

Step 3 For the top/bottom flying geese borders, sew together 7 flying geese units; press. Make 2 border strips. Sew the borders to the top/bottom edges of the quilt center; press.

Step 4 For the side flying geese borders, sew together 9 flying geese units; press. Make 2 border strips. Sew the 4-1/2-inch **GREEN** corner squares to both ends of the border strips; press. Sew the borders to the side edges of the quilt center; press.

Step 5 Attach the 8-1/2-inch wide **BLUE** outer border strips.

Putting It All Together

Cut the 7-1/8 yard length of backing fabric in thirds crosswise to make 3, 2-3/8 yard lengths. Refer to *Finishing the Quilt* on page 159 for complete instructions.

Binding

Cutting

From **GOLD PLAID**:

- Cut enough 2-3/4-inch wide **bias** strips to make a 360-inch long strip.

Sew the binding to the quilt using a 3/8-inch seam allowance. This measurement will produce a 1/2-inch wide finished double binding. Refer to **Binding** and **Diagonal Piecing** on page 159 for complete instructions.

Sunshine Patches Throw
80 x 96-inches

*Soft summer shades of blue and beige blend
with gold in a generously-sized patchwork quilt
that showcases the beautiful quilting detail.*

Blueberries & Cream

Quilt

86 x 103-inches

Fabrics and Supplies

1 yard **BLUE PRINT #1** for blocks

1-1/2 yards **GOLD PRINT** for blocks
and middle border

4-7/8 yards **BEIGE PRINT** for blocks,
alternate blocks, and side and corner triangles

3-3/8 yards **BLUE PRINT #2** for blocks,
inner and outer borders

7/8 yard **GOLD PRINT** for binding

7-1/2 yards for backing

quilt batting, at least 92 x 109-inches

Pieced Blocks

Makes 20 blocks

Cutting

From **BLUE PRINT #1**:
- Cut 3, 4-1/2 x 42-inch strips. From the strips cut:
  20, 4-1/2-inch squares
- Cut 5, 2-1/2 x 42-inch strips. From the strips cut:
  80, 2-1/2-inch squares

From **GOLD PRINT**:
- Cut 14, 2-1/2 x 42-inch strips. From the strips cut:
  80, 2-1/2 x 4-1/2-inch rectangles
  80, 2-1/2-inch squares

From **BEIGE PRINT**:
- Cut 6, 2-7/8 x 42-inch strips
- Cut 19, 2-1/2 x 42-inch strips. From the strips cut:
  80, 2-1/2 x 4-1/2-inch rectangles
  160, 2-1/2-inch squares

From **BLUE PRINT #2**:
- Cut 6, 2-7/8 x 42-inch strips

Piecing

Step 1   Position a 2-1/2-inch **BEIGE** square on the
corner of a 2-1/2 x 4-1/2-inch **GOLD** rectangle.
Draw a diagonal line on the square and stitch on
the line. Trim the seam allowance to 1/4-inch;
press. Repeat this process at the opposite corner
of the rectangle. <u>At this point each unit should
measure 2-1/2 x 4-1/2-inches.</u>

Make 80

Step 2   Sew 2-1/2 x 4-1/2-inch **BEIGE** rectangles to the top edge of each of the Step 1 rectangles; press. Make 40 units. Sew the units to the top/bottom edges of each 4-1/2-inch **BLUE #1** square; press. <u>At this point each unit should measure 4-1/2 x 12-1/2-inches.</u>

Make 20

Step 3   With right sides together, layer the 2-7/8 x 42-inch **BEIGE** and **BLUE #2** strips together in pairs. Press together, but do not sew. Cut the layered strips into squares. Cut the layered squares in half diagonally to make 160 sets of triangles. Stitch 1/4-inch from the diagonal edge of each pair of triangles; press.

Crosscut 80, 2-7/8-inch squares

Make 160, 2-1/2-inch triangle-pieced squares

Step 4   Sew a 2-1/2-inch **BLUE #1** square to the left edge of 40 of the Step 3 triangle-pieced squares. Press the seam allowances toward the **BLUE** squares. Sew a 2-1/2-inch **GOLD** square to the right edge of the remaining 40 triangle-pieced squares. Press the seam allowances toward the **GOLD** squares. Sew the units together; press. <u>At this point each unit should measure 4-1/2-inches square.</u>

Make 80   *Make 80*

Make 80

Step 5   Sew the Step 4 units to the top/bottom edges of the remaining 4-1/2-inch Step 2 units; press. <u>At this point each unit should measure 4-1/2 x 12-1/2-inches.</u>

Make 40

Step 6   Sew the Step 5 units to both side edges of the Step 2 units; press. <u>At this point each block should measure 12-1/2-inches square.</u>

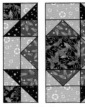

Make 20

Quilt Center

Note: *The side and corner triangles are larger than necessary and will be trimmed before the borders are added.*

Cutting

From **BEIGE PRINT**:

- Cut 2, 19 x 42-inch strips. From the strips cut: 4, 19-inch squares, cutting each square twice diagonally to make 16 triangles. You will be using only 14 for side triangles.
- Cut 4, 12-1/2 x 42-inch strips. From the strips cut: 12, 12-1/2-inch alternate block squares.
- Cut 1, 10 x 42-inch strip. From the strip cut: 2, 10-inch squares, cutting each square once diagonally to make 4 corner triangles.

Quilt Center Assembly

Step 1   Referring to the quilt diagram for block placement, sew together the pieced blocks, 12-1/2-inch square **BEIGE** alternate blocks, and **BEIGE** side triangles in 8 diagonal rows. Press the seam allowances toward the alternate blocks and side triangles.

Step 2   Pin the rows together at the block intersections; stitch together and press.

Step 3   Sew the **BEIGE** corner triangles to the quilt center; press.

Step 4   Trim away the excess fabric from the side and corner triangles taking care to allow a 1/4-inch seam allowance beyond the corners of each block. Refer to **Trimming Side and Corner Triangles** for complete instructions.

Borders

Note: *The yardage given allows for the border strips to be cut on the crosswise grain. Diagonally piece the strips as needed, referring to* **Diagonal Piecing** *instructions on page 159. Read through* **Border** *instructions on page 158 for general instructions on adding borders.*

Cutting

From **BLUE PRINT #2**:
   • Cut 11, 5-1/2 x 42-inch outer border strips
   • Cut 10, 3-1/2 x 42-inch inner border strips

From **GOLD PRINT**:
   • Cut 9, 1-1/2 x 42-inch middle border strips

Attaching the Borders

Step 1   Attach the 3-1/2-inch wide **BLUE #2** inner border strips.

Step 2   Attach the 1-1/2-inch wide **GOLD** middle border strips.

Step 3   Attach the 5-1/2-inch wide **BLUE #2** outer border strips.

Putting It All Together

Cut the 7-1/2 yard length of backing fabric in thirds crosswise to make 3, 2-1/2 yard lengths. Refer to *Finishing the Quilt* on page 159 for complete instructions.

Binding

Cutting

From **GOLD PRINT**:
   • Cut 10, 2-3/4 x 42-inch strips

Sew the binding to the quilt using a 3/8-inch seam allowance. This measurement will produce a 1/2-inch wide finished double binding. Refer to **Binding** and **Diagonal Piecing** instructions on page 159.

Trimming Side and Corner Triangles

Begin at a corner by lining up your ruler 1/4-inch beyond the points of the corners of the blocks as shown. Cut along the edge of the ruler. Repeat this procedure on all four sides of the quilt top.

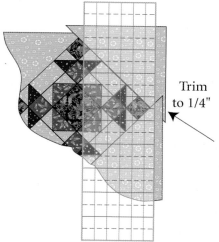

Trim to 1/4"

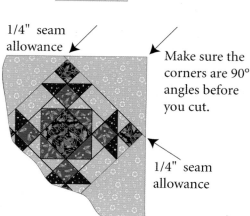

1/4" seam allowance

Make sure the corners are 90° angles before you cut.

1/4" seam allowance

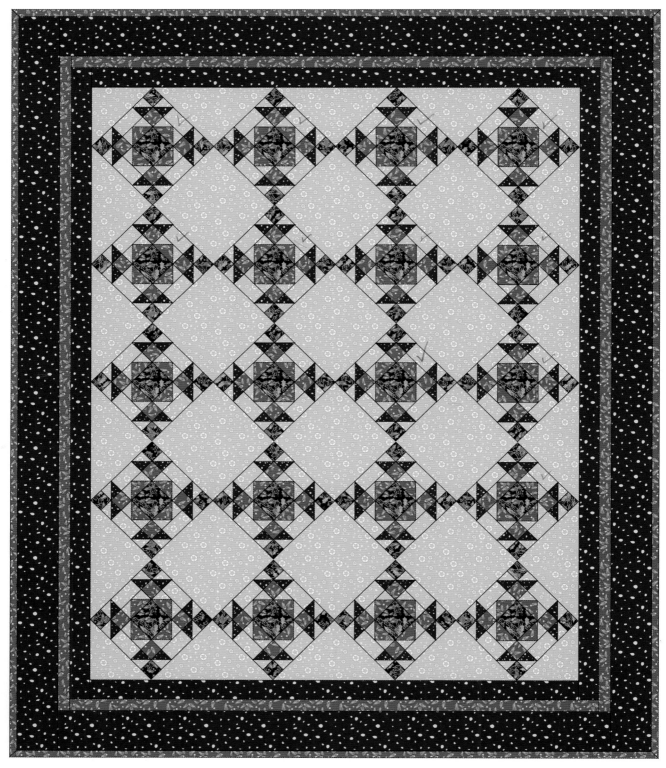

Blueberries & Cream Quilt
86 x 103-inches

Quilting Suggestions:

- Beige alternate blocks - TB18 Lady Slipper.
- Beige side triangles - TB40-12" Corner Swirl.
- Beige corner triangles - TB40-9" Corner Swirl.
- Pieced block - TB10 Radish Top.
- The three borders quilted as one - TB38 Pansy Vine.

The **THIMBLEBERRIES**® quilt stencils are by Quilting Creations International.

TB18 Lady Slipper Quilting Suggestion

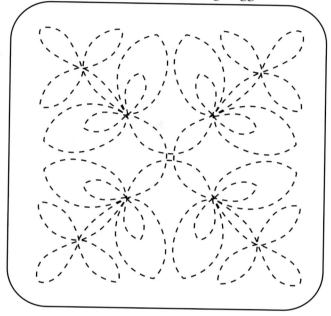

TB10 Radish Top Quilting Suggestion

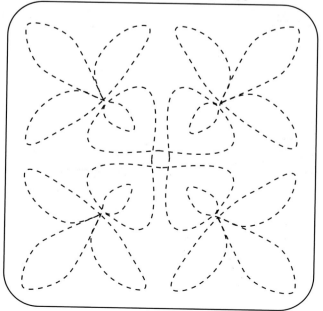

TB40 Corner Swirl Quilting Suggestion

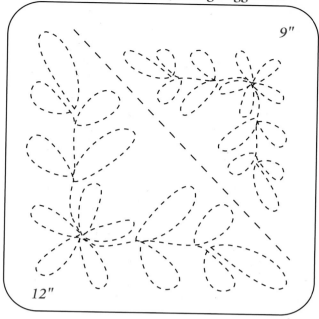

9"

12"

TB38 Pansy Vine Quilting Suggestion

House blocks have been a perennial favorite
of quilters for generations. The dramatic sawtooth
border draws the eye to the bold graphics in the quilt center.

Blue House

Wallhanging

36-inches square

Fabrics and Supplies

1-1/2 yards **BLUE PRINT** for house blocks, sawtooth border, middle border, and outer border

1 yard **BEIGE PRINT** for background, inner border, sawtooth border, and corner squares

3/8 yard **RED PLAID DIAGONAL PRINT** for binding

1-1/8 yards for backing

quilt batting, at least 42-inches square

House Blocks

Makes 4 blocks

Cutting

From **BLUE PRINT**:
- Cut 2, 2-7/8-inch squares
- Cut 2, 2-1/2 x 42-inch strips. From the strips cut:
  4, 2-1/2 x 4-1/2-inch rectangles
  12, 2-1/2-inch squares
- Cut 4, 1-1/2 x 42-inch strips. From the strips cut:
  8, 1-1/2 x 6-1/2-inch rectangles
  8, 1-1/2 x 5-1/2-inch rectangles
  12, 1-1/2 x 2-1/2-inch rectangles
  8, 1-1/2-inch squares

From **BEIGE PRINT**:
- Cut 2, 2-7/8-inch squares
- Cut 2, 2-1/2 x 42-inch strips. From the strips cut:
  8, 2-1/2 x 3-1/2-inch rectangles
  8, 2-1/2-inch squares
- Cut 3, 1-1/2 x 42-inch strips. From the strips cut:
  4, 1-1/2 x 6-1/2-inch rectangles
  4, 1-1/2 x 4-1/2-inch rectangles
  4, 1-1/2 x 3-1/2-inch rectangles
  12, 1-1/2 x 2-1/2-inch rectangles

Piecing

Step 1 Sew together 2 of the 1-1/2-inch **BLUE** squares, 2 of the 1-1/2 x 2-1/2-inch **BEIGE** rectangles, and 1 of the 1-1/2 x 3-1/2-inch **BEIGE** rectangles; press. <u>At this point each section should measure 1-1/2 x 9-1/2-inches.</u>

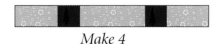

Make 4

right sides together, layer the 2-7/8-inch
BLUE and **BEIGE** squares together in pairs. Press
together, but do not sew. Cut the layered squares
in half diagonally to make 4 sets of triangles. Stitch
1/4-inch from the diagonal edge of each pair of
triangles; press. At this point each triangle-pieced
square should measure 2-1/2-inches square.

*Make 4, 2-1/2-inch
triangle-pieced squares*

Step 3 With right sides together, position a 2-1/2-inch
BLUE square on the right corner of a
2-1/2 x 3-1/2-inch **BEIGE** rectangle. Draw a
diagonal line on the square; stitch on the line. Trim
the seam allowance to 1/4-inch; press. Repeat this
process at the opposite corner of the rectangle.

Make 4

Step 4 With right sides together, position a 2-1/2-inch
BEIGE square on the right corner of a
2-1/2 x 4-1/2-inch **BLUE** rectangle. Draw a
diagonal line on the square; stitch, trim, and press.

Make 4

Step 5 Sew together the Step 2, Step 3, and Step 4 units;
press. At this point each section should measure
2-1/2 x 9-1/2-inches.

Make 4

Step 6 Sew together 2 of the 1-1/2 x 2-1/2-inch
BLUE rectangles, a 1-1/2 x 2-1/2-inch **BEIGE**
rectangle, and a 2-1/2 x 3-1/2-inch **BEIGE**
rectangle; press. Sew 1-1/2 x 6-1/2-inch **BLUE**

rectangles to both side edges of the unit; press. Sew
a 1-1/2 x 6-1/2-inch **BEIGE** rectangle to the right
edge of the unit; press. At this point each unit
should measure 5-1/2 x 6-1/2-inches.

Make 4

Step 7 Sew together a 1-1/2 x 2-1/2-inch **BLUE** rectangle,
a 2-1/2-inch **BEIGE** square, and a 2-1/2-inch
BLUE square; press. Sew 1-1/2 x 5-1/2-inch **BLUE**
rectangles to both side edges of the unit; press. Sew
a 1-1/2 x 4-1/2-inch **BEIGE** rectangle to the top
edge of this unit; press. At this point each unit
should measure 4-1/2 x 6-1/2-inches.

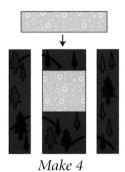

Make 4

Step 8 Sew together the Step 6 and Step 7 units; press.
At this point each section should measure
6-1/2 x 9-1/2-inches.

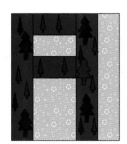 

Make 4

Step 9 Referring to the block diagram, sew together the Step 1, Step 5, and Step 8 sections; press. <u>At this point each block should measure 9-1/2-inches square.</u>

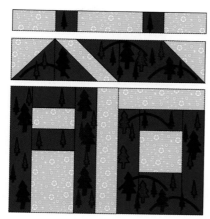

Make 4

Quilt Center

Cutting

From **BEIGE PRINT**:

- Cut 1, 2-1/2 x 42-inch strip. From the strip cut:
  1, 2-1/2 x 20-1/2-inch lattice strip
  2, 2-1/2 x 9-1/2-inch lattice strips

Quilt Center Assembly

Referring to the quilt diagram for placement, sew a house block to both side edges of a 2-1/2 x 9-1/2-inch **BEIGE** lattice strip; press. Make 2 block rows. Sew the block rows to both side edges of the 2-1/2 x 20-1/2-inch **BEIGE** lattice strip; press. <u>At this point the quilt center should measure 20-1/2-inches square.</u>

Borders

Note: *The yardage given allows for the border strips to be cut on the crosswise grain. Diagonally piece the strips as needed, referring to* **Diagonal Piecing** *instructions on page 159. Read through* **Border** *instructions on page 158 for general instructions on adding borders.*

Cutting

From **BLUE PRINT**:

- Cut 4, 3-1/2 x 42-inch outer border strips
- Cut 3, 1-7/8 x 42-inch strips
- Cut 3, 1-1/2 x 42-inch middle border strips

From **BEIGE PRINT**:

- Cut 3, 2-1/2 x 42-inch inner border strips
- Cut 4, 2-1/2-inch corner squares
- Cut 3, 1-7/8 x 42-inch strips

Assembling and Attaching the Borders

Step 1 Attach the 2-1/2-inch wide **BEIGE** inner border strips.

Step 2 With right sides together, layer the 1-7/8 x 42-inch **BLUE** and **BEIGE** strips in pairs. Press together, but do not sew. Cut the layered strips into squares. Cut the layered squares in half diagonally to make 96 sets of triangles. Stitch 1/4-inch from the diagonal edge of each pair of triangles; press.

Crosscut 48, 1-7/8-inch squares   *Make 96, 1-1/2-inch triangle-pieced squares*

Step 3 For the sawtooth borders, sew together 24 of the triangle-pieced squares; press. Make 4 sawtooth borders. <u>At this point each sawtooth border strip should measure 1-1/2 x 24-1/2-inches.</u>

Note: *If the completed sawtooth border is too long or too short, adjust seams in many places rather than trying to make up the difference in just a few places. You must match the center of the border to the center of the quilt and adjust the seams going in either direction.*

Step 4 Cut the 1-1/2-inch wide **BLUE** middle border strips to the length of the sawtooth border strips; sew the **BLUE** strips to the sawtooth borders; press. Sew the border strips to the top/bottom edges of the quilt center; press. Sew 2-1/2-inch **BEIGE** corner squares to the ends of the remaining sawtooth/middle border strips; press.

Sew the border strips to the side edges of the quilt center; press. <u>At this point the quilt center should measure 28-1/2-inches square.</u>

Step 5 Attach the 3-1/2-inch wide **BLUE** outer border strips.

Putting It All Together

Trim the backing and batting so they are about 6-inches larger than the quilt top. Refer to *Finishing the Quilt* on page 159 for complete instructions.

Binding

Cutting

From **RED PLAID DIAGONAL PRINT**:
• Cut 4, 2-3/4 x 42-inch strips

Sew the binding to the quilt using a 3/8-inch seam allowance. This measurement will produce a 1/2-inch wide finished double binding. Refer to *Binding* and *Diagonal Piecing* instructions on page 159.

The bold graphics of the house block and the dramatic border make this simple quilt just as stunning in red and beige as it is in blue and beige.

Blue House Wallhanging
36-inches square

*Tone on tone fabric choices and clean, crisp lines
create a striking contemporary look,
yet maintain an overall feeling of warmth and serenity.*

City Block

Quilt

88 x 104-inches

Fabrics and Supplies

3-3/8 yards **DARK BEIGE PRINT** for quilt center (cut on the crosswise grain) and middle borders (cut on the lengthwise grain)

3-5/8 yards **BEIGE PRINT #1** for quilt center (cut on the crosswise grain) and outer borders (cut on the lengthwise grain)

5/8 yard **CREAM PRINT** for quilt center and pieced border

1-1/2 yards **BEIGE PRINT #2** for inner border, pieced border, and middle border

1-5/8 yards **BEIGE PRINT #3** for pieced border and middle border

1 yard **BEIGE PRINT #1** for binding

7-7/8 yards for backing

quilt batting, at least 94 x 110-inches

Quilt Center

Cutting

From **DARK BEIGE PRINT:**

> *Note: Cut the 3-3/8 yard length crosswise into:*
> *1, 5/8 yard length and*
> *1, 2-2/3 yard length. <u>Set the 2-2/3 yard length aside for the middle border.</u>*

From the 5/8 yard length:
- Cut 1, 12-1/2 x 42-inch strip. From the strip cut:
  1, 12-1/2-inch center square
  4, 6-1/2 x 12-1/2-inch rectangles
- Cut 1, 6-1/2 x 42-inch strip. From the strip cut:
  4, 6-1/2-inch squares

From **BEIGE PRINT #1:**

> *Note: Cut the 3-5/8 yard length crosswise into:*
> *1, 5/8 yard length and*
> *1, 3 yard length. <u>Set the 3 yard length aside for the outer border.</u>*

From the 5/8 yard length:
- Cut 3, 6-1/2 x 42-inch strips. From the strips cut:
  4, 6-1/2 x 12-1/2-inch rectangles
  8, 6-1/2-inch squares

From **CREAM PRINT:**
- Cut 1, 6-1/2 x 42-inch strip. From the strip cut:
  4, 6-1/2-inch squares

Quilt Center Assembly

Referring to the quilt center assembly diagram for placement, lay out the **DARK BEIGE** squares and rectangles, the 6-1/2-inch **CREAM** squares, and the **BEIGE #1** squares and rectangles. Sew the pieces together in rows. Press the seam allowances toward the **BEIGE #1** squares and rectangles. Sew the rows together; press. <u>At this point the quilt center should measure 36-inches square.</u>

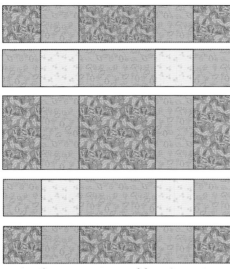

Quilt Center Assembly Diagram

Borders

*Note: The yardage given allows for the **BEIGE #2**, **BEIGE #3**, and **CREAM** border strips to be cut on the <u>crosswise grain</u>. The yardage given allows for the **DARK BEIGE** and **BEIGE #1** border strips to be cut on the <u>lengthwise grain</u> (a couple extra inches are allowed for trimming). Cutting the strips on the <u>lengthwise grain</u> will eliminate the need for piecing the wide strips. Read through **Border** instructions on page 158 for general instructions on adding borders.*

Cutting

From **BEIGE PRINT #2**:
- Cut 4, 4-1/2 x 42-inch strips
- Cut 4, 2-1/2 x 42-inch inner border strips
- Cut 9, 2-1/2 x 42-inch middle border strips

From **BEIGE PRINT #3**:
- Cut 6, 4-1/2 x 42-inch strips
- Cut 9, 2-1/2 x 42-inch middle border strips
- Cut 2, 2-1/2 x 4-1/2-inch rectangles

From **CREAM PRINT**:
- Cut 2, 4-1/2 x 42-inch strips
- Cut 4, 2-1/2-inch squares

From **DARK BEIGE PRINT**:
- Cut 2, 6-1/2 x 84-inch side second middle border strips
- Cut 2, 6-1/2 x 55-inch top/bottom first middle border strips
- Cut 2, 6-1/2 x 55-inch top/bottom second middle border strips

From **BEIGE PRINT #1**:
- Cut 2, 8-1/2 x 108-inch side outer border strips
- Cut 2, 8-1/2 x 75-inch top/bottom outer border strips

Assembling and Attaching the Borders

Step 1   Attach the 2-1/2-inch wide **BEIGE #2** inner border strips.

Step 2   Aligning long edges, sew the 4-1/2 x 42-inch **CREAM** strips and 2 of the 4-1/2 x 42-inch **BEIGE #3** strips together in pairs. Make 2 strip sets. Press, referring to ***Hints and Helps for Pressing Strip Sets*** on page 158. Cut the strip sets into segments.

Crosscut 20, 2-1/2-inch wide segments

Step 3   For the top/bottom pieced borders, sew together 4 of the Step 2 segments. Sew a 2-1/2 x 4-1/2-inch **BEIGE #3** rectangle to the right edge. Sew a 2-1/2-inch **CREAM** square to both ends of the strip; press. Make 2 border strips. <u>At this point each pieced border strip should measure 2-1/2 x 40-1/2-inches.</u> Sew the border strips to the top/bottom edges of the quilt center; press.

Make 2

Step 4 For the side pieced borders, sew together 6 of the Step 2 segments. Remove a 2-1/2 x 4-1/2-inch **BEIGE #3** rectangle from the end of the strip; press. Make 2 border strips. <u>At this point each pieced border strip should measure 2-1/2 x 44-1/2-inches.</u> Sew the border strips to the side edges of the quilt center; press.

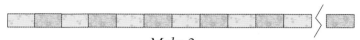

Make 2

Step 5 Aligning long edges, sew 3 of the 4-1/2 x 42-inch **BEIGE #2** strips and 3 of the 4-1/2 x 42-inch **BEIGE #3** strips together in pairs; press. Make 3 strip sets. Cut the strip sets into segments.

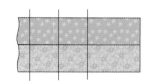

Crosscut 26, 4-1/2-inch wide segments

Step 6 For the top/bottom pieced borders, sew together 6 of the Step 5 segments. Remove a 4-1/2-inch **BEIGE #2** square from the end of the strip; press. Make 2 border strips. <u>At this point each pieced border strip should measure 4-1/2 x 44-1/2-inches.</u> Sew the border strips to the top/bottom edges of the quilt center; press.

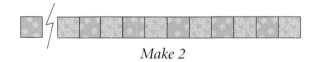

Make 2

Step 7 For the side pieced borders, sew together 7 of the Step 5 segments. Remove a 4-1/2-inch **BEIGE #3** square from the end of the strip; press. Make 2 border strips. <u>At this point each pieced border strip should measure 4-1/2 x 52-1/2-inches.</u> Sew the border strips to the side edges of the quilt center; press.

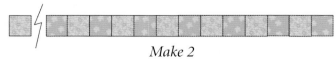

Make 2

Step 8 Attach the 6-1/2 x 55-inch **DARK BEIGE** top/bottom first middle border strips.

Step 9 Aligning long edges, sew the remaining 4-1/2 x 42-inch **BEIGE #2** and **BEIGE #3** strips together; press. Make 1 strip set. Cut the strip set into segments.

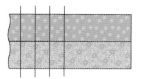

Crosscut 14, 2-1/2-inch wide segments

Step 10 For the top/bottom pieced borders, sew together 7 of the Step 9 segments. Remove a 2-1/2 x 4-1/2-inch **BEIGE #3** rectangle from the end of the strip; press. Make 2 border strips. <u>At this point each pieced border strip should measure 2-1/2 x 52-1/2-inches.</u> Sew the border strips to the top/bottom edges of the quilt center; press.

Make 2

Step 11 Attach the 6-1/2 x 55-inch **DARK BEIGE** top/bottom second middle border strips.

Step 12 Attach the 6-1/2 x 84-inch **DARK BEIGE** side middle border strips.

Step 13 Attach the 2-1/2-inch wide **BEIGE #2** middle border strips.

Step 14 Attach the 2-1/2-inch wide **BEIGE #3** middle border strips.

Step 15 Attach the 8-1/2 x 75-inch **BEIGE #1** top/bottom outer border strips.

Step 16 Attach the 8-1/2 x 108-inch **BEIGE #1** side outer border strips.

Putting It All Together

Cut the 7-7/8 yard length of backing fabric in thirds crosswise to make 3, 2-5/8 yard lengths. Refer to *Finishing the Quilt* on page 159 for complete instructions.

Binding

Cutting

From **BEIGE PRINT #1**:
- Cut 10, 2-3/4 x 42-inch strips

Sew the binding to the quilt using a 3/8-inch seam allowance. This measurement will produce a 1/2-inch wide finished double binding. Refer to **Binding** and **Diagonal Piecing** on page 159 for complete instructions.

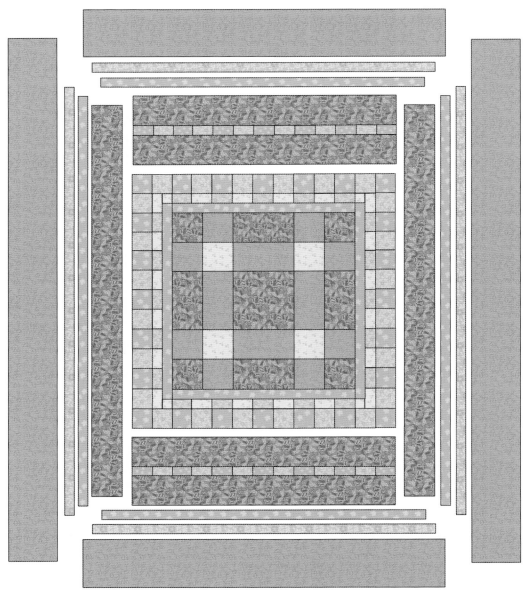

Border Assembly Diagram

City Block Quilt

88 x 104-inches

A dozen delightful floral blocks make up this seasonal salute to summer. Bringing the lilies of the field into the bedroom creates an inviting and restful garden-themed retreat.

Summer Lily

Quilt

80 x 100-inches

Fabrics and Supplies

1-2/3 yards **RED PRINT** for flowers

2 yards **GREEN PRINT** for leaves, stems, center squares, and lattice post squares

4-3/4 yards **BEIGE PRINT** for background and lattice segments

3/4 yard **BLUE PRINT** for inner border

2-1/4 yards **GREEN/ROSE FLORAL** for outer border

1 yard **BLUE PRINT** for binding

7-1/8 yards for backing

quilt batting, at least 86 x 106-inches

Lily Blocks

Makes 12 blocks

Cutting

From **RED PRINT**:
- Cut 2, 2-7/8 x 42-inch strips
- Cut 12, 2-1/2 x 42-inch strips.
  From the strips cut:
  192, 2-1/2-inch squares
- Cut 6 more 2-1/2 x 42-inch strips.
  From the strips cut:
  48, 2-1/2 x 4-1/2-inch rectangles

From **GREEN PRINT**:
- Cut 2, 4-1/2 x 42-inch strips. From the strips cut:
  12, 4-1/2-inch squares
- Cut 2, 2-7/8 x 42-inch strips
- Cut 9, 2-1/2 x 42-inch strips. From the strips cut:
  144, 2-1/2-inch squares
- Cut 5, 1 x 42-inch strips. From the strips cut:
  48, 1 x 4-inch strips

From **BEIGE PRINT**:
- Cut 6, 4-1/2 x 42-inch strips. From the strips cut:
  48, 4-1/2-inch squares
- Cut 4, 2-5/8 x 42-inch strips. From the strips cut:
  48, 2-5/8-inch squares. Cut the squares in half diagonally to make 96 triangles.
- Cut 3, 2-1/2 x 42-inch strips. From the strips cut:
  48, 2-1/2-inch squares
- Cut 18 more 2-1/2 x 42-inch strips.
  From the strips cut:
  144, 2-1/2 x 4-1/2-inch rectangles

Piecing

Step 1 With right sides together, position a 2-1/2-inch **RED** square on the corner of a 2-1/2 x 4-1/2-inch **BEIGE** rectangle. Draw a diagonal line on the square and stitch on the line. Trim the seam allowance to 1/4-inch; press. Repeat this process at the opposite corner of the rectangle.

Make 96

Step 2 With right sides together, position a 2-1/2-inch **GREEN** square on the right corner of a 2-1/2 x 4-1/2-inch **RED** rectangle. Draw a diagonal line on the square; stitch, trim, and press. Sew these units to the bottom edge of 24 of the Step 1 units; press.

Make 24

Make 24

Step 3 With right sides together, position a 2-1/2-inch **GREEN** square on the left corner of a 2-1/2 x 4-1/2-inch **RED** rectangle. Draw a diagonal line on the square; stitch, trim, and press. Sew these units to the bottom edge of 24 of the Step 1 units; press.

Make 24

Make 24

Step 4 With right sides together, position a 2-1/2-inch **GREEN** square on the upper left corner of a 4-1/2-inch **BEIGE** square. Draw a diagonal line on the **GREEN** square; stitch, trim, and press. Repeat this process at the upper right corner of the **BEIGE** square. Sew 24 of the 2-1/2 x 4-1/2-inch **BEIGE** rectangles to the top edge of 24 of the units; press.

Make 24 *Make 24*

Step 5 Referring to the diagram, sew 24 of the Step 4 units to the top/bottom edges of the 4-1/2-inch **GREEN** squares; press. <u>At this point each center unit should measure 4-1/2 x 16-1/2-inches.</u>

Make 12

Step 6 With right sides together, layer the 2-7/8 x 42-inch **RED** and **GREEN** strips in pairs. Press together, but do not sew. Cut the layered strips into squares. Cut the layered squares in half diagonally to make 48 sets of triangles. Stitch 1/4-inch from the diagonal edge of each pair of triangles; press.

Crosscut 24, 2-7/8-inch squares

Make 48, 2-1/2-inch triangle-pieced squares

Step 7 To make a stem unit, center a **BEIGE** triangle on a 1 x 4-inch **GREEN** strip; stitch together with a 1/4-inch seam allowance. Center another **BEIGE** triangle on the opposite edge of the **GREEN** strip; stitch. Press the seam allowances toward the **GREEN** strip. Trim the stem unit so it measures 2-1/2-inches square.

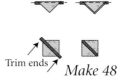

Trim ends *Make 48*

Step 8 Sew 24 of the stem units to the right edge of 24 of the triangle-pieced squares; press. Sew the units to the bottom edge of the Step 2 units; press. <u>At this point each unit should measure 4-1/2 x 6-1/2-inches.</u>

Make 24 *Make 24*

Step 9 Sew 24 of the stem units to the left edge of the remaining 24 triangle-pieced squares; press. Sew the units to the bottom edge of the Step 3 units; press. <u>At this point each unit should measure 4-1/2 x 6-1/2-inches.</u>

Make 24   *Make 24*

Step 10 Referring to the diagram for placement, sew the Step 8 and Step 9 units to the edges of the remaining Step 4 units; press. <u>At this point each unit should measure 4-1/2 x 16-1/2-inches.</u>

 Step 8

 Step 9

Make 24

Step 11 Sew together 2 of the Step 1 units, 1 of the 2-1/2 x 4-1/2-inch **BEIGE** rectangles, and 2 of the 2-1/2-inch **BEIGE** squares; press. <u>At this point each unit should measure 2-1/2 x 16-1/2-inches.</u>

Make 24

Step 12 Referring to the block diagrams for placement, lay out the Step 5, 10, and 11 units in 5 vertical rows for each block. Sew the units together to make each lily block; press. <u>At this point each lily block should measure 16-1/2-inches square.</u>

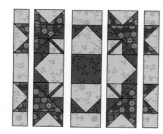 

Make 12

Quilt Center

Cutting

From **BEIGE PRINT**:

- Cut 16, 4-1/2 x 42-inch strips. From the strips cut: 31, 4-1/2 x 16-1/2-inch lattice segments

From **GREEN PRINT**:

- Cut 3, 4-1/2 x 42-inch strips. From the strips cut: 20, 4-1/2-inch lattice post squares

Quilt Center Assembly

Step 1 Sew together 3 of the 4-1/2 x 16-1/2-inch **BEIGE** lattice segments and 4 of the 4-1/2-inch **GREEN** lattice post squares. Press the seam allowances toward the **BEIGE** lattice segments. <u>At this point each lattice strip should measure 4-1/2 x 64-1/2-inches.</u>

Make 5 lattice strips

Step 2 Sew together 3 of the lily blocks and 4 of the 4-1/2 x 16-1/2-inch **BEIGE** lattice segments. Press the seam allowances toward the **BEIGE** lattice segments. <u>At this point each block row should measure 16-1/2 x 64-1/2-inches.</u>

Make 4 block rows

Step 3 Referring to the quilt diagram, sew the block rows and lattice strips together; press. <u>At this point the quilt center should measure 64-1/2 x 84-1/2-inches.</u>

Borders

Note: *The yardage given allows for the border strips to be cut on the crosswise grain. Diagonally piece the strips as needed, referring to* **Diagonal Piecing** *instructions on page 159. Read through* **Border** *instructions on page 158 for general instructions on adding borders.*

Cutting

From **BLUE PRINT**:
- Cut 8, 2-1/2 x 42-inch inner border strips

From **GREEN/ROSE FLORAL**:
- Cut 10, 6-1/2 x 42-inch outer border strips

Attaching the Borders

Step 1 Attach the 2-1/2-inch wide **BLUE** inner border strips.

Step 2 Attach the 6-1/2-inch wide **GREEN/ROSE FLORAL** outer border strips.

Putting It All Together

Cut the 7-1/8 yard length of backing fabric in thirds crosswise to make 3, 2-3/8 yard lengths. Refer to **Finishing the Quilt** on page 159 for complete instructions.

Binding

Cutting

From **BLUE PRINT**:
- Cut 10, 2-3/4 x 42-inch strips

Sew the binding to the quilt using a 3/8-inch seam allowance. This measurement will produce a 1/2-inch wide finished double binding. Refer to **Binding** and **Diagonal Piecing** on page 159 for complete instructions.

Summer Lily Quilt

80 x 100-inches

*Tall pine, woodland flower and midnight star blocks
are reminders of adventures collected while
walking through the woods on a moonlit evening.*

Nature Walk

Wallhanging
58 x 64-inches

Fabrics and Supplies

1/4 yard **RED PRINT #1**
for stone walk units

1-3/4 yards **BEIGE PRINT** for background

1/3 yard **BLUE PRINT** for firefly blocks and
woodland flower block

1/4 yard **GREEN PRINT #1** for tall pine
blocks

1/3 yard **GREEN PRINT #2** for tall pine
blocks and shoo fly block

1/8 yard **GREEN PRINT #3**
for tall pine blocks

1/4 yard **BROWN PRINT**
for tall pine blocks, turning leaf blocks,
and shoo fly block

1/4 yard **LIGHT GOLD PRINT**
or midnight star blocks
and woodland flower block

1/3 yard **DARK GOLD PRINT** for
midnight star blocks and shoo fly block

1/4 yard **BLACK PRINT #1** for midnight
star blocks and shoo fly block

1/3 yard **RED PRINT #2** for turning leaf
blocks and shoo fly block

1/4 yard **GREEN PRINT #4**
for turning leaf blocks

1/3 yard **RED PRINT #3**
for woodland flower block

1/4 yard **GOLD FLORAL**
for woodland flower block

1/2 yard **CHESTNUT PRINT**
for inner border

should have
1-3/8 yards **BLACK PRINT #2**
for outer border

7/8 yard **MULTICOLOR PLAID**
for binding (cut on the bias)

3-3/4 yards for backing

quilt batting, at least 64 x 70-inches

Stone Walk

Makes 2 blocks

Cutting

From RED PRINT #1 and BEIGE PRINT:

- Cut 3, 2-1/2 x 42-inch strips from each fabric

Piecing

Step 1 Aligning long edges, sew 2-1/2 x 42-inch **RED #1** strips to both side edges of a 2-1/2 x 42-inch **BEIGE** strip; press. Cut the strip set into segments.

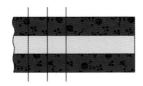

Crosscut 10, 2-1/2-inch wide segments

Step 2 Aligning long edges, sew 2-1/2 x 42-inch **BEIGE** strips to both side edges of a 2-1/2 x 42-inch **RED #1** strip; press. Cut the strip set into segments.

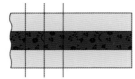

Crosscut 10, 2-1/2-inch wide segments

Step 3 Referring to the diagram for placement, sew together 5 of the Step 1 segments and 4 of the Step 2 segments; press. Make 2 stone walk units. <u>At this point each unit should measure 6-1/2 x 18-1/2-inches.</u>

Make 2

Firefly

Makes 12 blocks

Cutting

From BLUE PRINT:

- Cut 1, 5-1/4 x 42-inch strip. From the strip cut: 6, 5-1/4-inch squares, cutting each square twice diagonally to make 24 triangles

From BEIGE PRINT:

- Cut 1, 5-1/4 x 42-inch strip. From the strip cut: 6, 5-1/4-inch squares, cutting each square twice diagonally to make 24 triangles
- Cut 1, 2-1/2 x 12-1/2-inch spacer strip

Piecing

Step 1 Layer the **BEIGE** and **BLUE** triangles in pairs. Stitch along the same bias edge of each set of layered triangles being careful not to stretch the triangles. Press the seam allowances toward the **BLUE** triangles. Make 24 triangle units. Sew the triangle units together in pairs; press. <u>At this point each firefly block should measure 4-1/2-inches square.</u>

bias edges   *Make 24*   *Make 12*

Step 2 Referring to the diagram for placement, sew together the firefly blocks in 3 rows of 4 blocks each; press. Sew the rows together; press. <u>At this point the firefly unit should measure 12-1/2 x 16-1/2-inches.</u> Sew the 2-1/2 x 12-1/2-inch **BEIGE** spacer strip to the right edge of the firefly unit; press.

Step 3 Sew the stone walk units to the top/bottom edges of the firefly unit; press. <u>At this point the unit should measure 18-1/2 x 24-1/2-inches.</u>

Tall Pine

Makes 2 blocks

Cutting

From GREEN PRINT #1:

- Cut 1, 4-1/2 x 42-inch strip. From the strip cut:
  - 2, 4-1/2 x 8-1/2-inch rectangles
  - 2, 2-1/2 x 8-1/2-inch rectangles
- Cut 4, 2-1/2 x 8-1/2-inch rectangles

From GREEN PRINT #2:

- Cut 8, 2-1/2 x 8-1/2-inch rectangles

From GREEN PRINT #3:

- Cut 4, 2-1/2 x 8-1/2-inch rectangles

From BROWN PRINT:

- Cut 2, 2-1/2-inch squares

From BEIGE PRINT:

- Cut 1, 4-1/2 x 42-inch strip. From the strip cut:
  - 4, 4-1/2-inch squares
  - 4, 2-1/2 x 3-1/2-inch rectangles
- Cut 3, 2-1/2 x 42-inch strips. From the strips cut:
  - 1, 2-1/2 x 24-1/2-inch spacer strip
  - 36, 2-1/2-inch squares

Piecing

Step 1 With right sides together, position a 4-1/2-inch **BEIGE** square on the corner of a 4-1/2 x 8-1/2-inch **GREEN #1** rectangle. Draw a diagonal line on the square and stitch on the line. Trim the seam allowance to 1/4-inch; press. Repeat this process at the opposite corner of the rectangle.

Make 2

Step 2 With right sides together, position 2-1/2-inch **BEIGE** squares on the corners of a 2-1/2 x 8-1/2-inch **GREEN #1** rectangle. Draw a diagonal line on the square; stitch, trim, and press. Repeat this process using the **GREEN #2** and **GREEN #3**, 2-1/2 x 8-1/2-inch rectangles.

| *Make 6* | *Make 8* | *Make 4* |
| GREEN #1 | GREEN #2 | GREEN #3 |

Step 3 Sew 2-1/2 x 3-1/2-inch **BEIGE** rectangles to both side edges of a 2-1/2-inch **BROWN** square; press.

Make 2

Step 4 Referring to the block diagram for color placement, sew the Step 1, 2, and 3 units together to make 2 tall pine blocks; press. <u>At this point each block should measure 8-1/2 x 24-1/2-inches.</u>

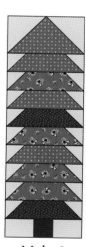

Step 5 Referring to the quilt center assembly diagram, sew the tall pine blocks to both long edges of the 2-1/2 x 24-1/2-inch **BEIGE** spacer strip; press. <u>At this point the unit should measure 18-1/2 x 24-1/2-inches.</u>

Make 2

Midnight Star

Makes 2 blocks

Cutting

From LIGHT GOLD PRINT:

- Cut 2, 4-1/2-inch squares

From BLACK PRINT #1:

- Cut 16, 2-1/2-inch squares

From DARK GOLD PRINT:

- Cut 2, 2-1/2 x 42-inch strips. From the strips cut:
  - 8, 2-1/2 x 4-1/2-inch rectangles
  - 16, 2-1/2-inch squares

From **BEIGE PRINT**:
- Cut 1, 4-1/2 x 42-inch strip. From the strip cut: 8, 4-1/2-inch squares
- Cut 1, 2-1/2 x 42-inch strip. From the strip cut: 8, 2-1/2 x 4-1/2-inch rectangles

Piecing

Step 1 With right sides together, position a 2-1/2-inch **BLACK #1** square on the corner of a 2-1/2 x 4-1/2 **DARK GOLD** rectangle. Draw a diagonal line on the square; stitch, trim, and press. Repeat this process on the opposite corner of the rectangle.

Make 8

Step 2 With right sides together, position a 2-1/2-inch **DARK GOLD** square on the corner of a 2-1/2 x 4-1/2-inch **BEIGE** rectangle. Draw a diagonal line on the square; stitch, trim, and press. Repeat this process on the opposite corner of the rectangle. Sew the units to the top edge of the Step 1 units; press.

Make 8   (*Make 8*)

Step 3 Sew 4-1/2-inch **BEIGE** squares to both side edges of 4 of the Step 2 units; press. Sew the remaining Step 2 units to both side edges of the 4-1/2-inch **LIGHT GOLD** squares; press. Referring to the block assembly diagram, sew the units together to make 2 midnight star blocks; press. <u>At this point each block should measure 12-1/2-inches square.</u>

Make 4

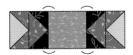
Make 2

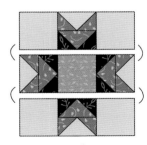
Make 2

Turning Leaf

Makes 2 blocks

Cutting

From **RED PRINT #2**:
- Cut 1, 4-7/8 x 42-inch strip. From the strip cut:
  4, 4-7/8-inch squares
  2, 4-1/2-inch squares

From **BEIGE PRINT**:
- Cut 1, 4-7/8 x 42-inch strip. From the strip cut:
  4, 4-7/8-inch squares
  2, 4-1/4-inch squares, cutting each square once in half diagonally to make 4 triangles

From **GREEN PRINT #4**:
- Cut 1, 4-1/2 x 42-inch strip. From the strip cut:
  2, 4-1/2 x 8-1/2-inch rectangles
  2, 4-1/2-inch squares

From **BROWN PRINT**:
- Cut 2, 1-1/2 x 7-inch strips

Piecing

Step 1 With right sides together, layer the 4-7/8-inch **RED #2** and **BEIGE** squares in pairs. Press together, but do not sew. Cut the layered squares in half diagonally to make 8 sets of triangles. Stitch 1/4-inch from the diagonal edge of each pair of triangles; press.

Make 8, 4-1/2-inch triangle-pieced squares

Step 2 To make a stem unit, center a **BEIGE** triangle on a 1-1/2 x 7-inch **BROWN** strip; stitch with a 1/4-inch seam. Center another **BEIGE** triangle on the opposite edge of the **BROWN** strip; stitch and press. Trim the stem unit so it measures 4-1/2-inches square.

Trim ends

Make 2

Step 3 Sew together 2 of the Step 1 triangle-pieced squares and a 4-1/2-inch **RED #2** square; press. Sew together a 4-1/2 x 8-1/2-inch **GREEN #4** rectangle and a triangle-pieced square; press. Sew together a stem unit, a 4-1/2-inch **GREEN #4** square, and a triangle-pieced square; press. Referring to the block assembly diagram, sew the units together to make 2 turning leaf blocks. <u>At this point each block should measure 12-1/2-inches square.</u>

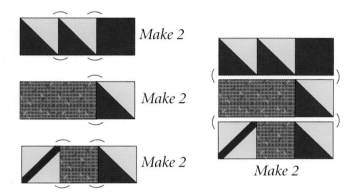

Make 2

Make 2

Make 2

Make 2

Step 4 Referring to the quilt center diagram, sew the midnight star and turning leaf blocks together in pairs; press. Sew the pairs together; press. <u>At this point the unit should measure 24-1/2-inches square.</u>

Shoo Fly

Makes 5 blocks

Cutting

From **DARK GOLD PRINT, BROWN PRINT, GREEN PRINT #2, BLACK PRINT #1,** and **RED PRINT #2**:

• Cut 1, 4-1/2-inch square from each fabric
• Cut 2, 2-7/8-inch squares from each fabric

From **BEIGE PRINT**:

• Cut 10, 2-7/8-inch squares
• Cut 3, 2-1/2 x 42-inch strips. From the strips cut:
20, 2-1/2 x 4-1/2-inch rectangles

Piecing

Step 1 With right sides together, layer the 2-7/8-inch **DARK GOLD** squares and 2 of the 2-7/8-inch **BEIGE** squares in pairs. Press together, but do not sew. Cut the layered squares in half diagonally to make 4 sets of triangles. Stitch 1/4-inch from the diagonal edge of each pair of triangles; press.

Make 4, 2-1/2-inch triangle-pieced squares

Step 2 Sew 2-1/2 x 4-1/2-inch **BEIGE** rectangles to both side edges of the 4-1/2-inch **DARK GOLD** square; press. Sew the Step 1 triangle-pieced squares to both side edges of the remaining 2-1/2 x 4-1/2-inch **BEIGE** rectangles; press. Sew the units together to make a shoo fly block. <u>At this point the shoo fly block should measure 8-1/2-inches square.</u>

Make 1

Step 3 Referring to the quilt center diagram, repeat Steps 1 and 2 using **BROWN, GREEN #2, BLACK #1,** and **RED #2** squares to make 1 shoo fly block each.

Woodland Flower

Makes 1 block

Cutting

From **LIGHT GOLD PRINT**:

• Cut 1, 4-1/2-inch square
• Cut 4, 2-1/2-inch squares

From **BLUE PRINT**:

• Cut 1, 2-1/2 x 42-inch strip. From the strip cut:
2, 2-1/2 x 8-1/2-inch rectangles
2, 2-1/2 x 4-1/2-inch rectangles
4, 1-1/2-inch squares

From **RED PRINT #3**:
- Cut 2, 2-7/8-inch squares
- Cut 2, 2-1/2 x 42-inch strips. From the strips cut:
  12, 2-1/2 x 4-1/2-inch rectangles
  4, 2-1/2-inch squares

From **GOLD FLORAL**:
- Cut 2, 2-1/2 x 42-inch strips. From the strips cut:
  4, 2-1/2 x 4-1/2-inch rectangles
  16, 2-1/2-inch squares

From **BEIGE PRINT**:
- Cut 2, 2-7/8-inch squares
- Cut 16, 2-1/2-inch squares

Piecing

Step 1 With right sides together, position 1-1/2-inch **BLUE** squares on each corner of the 4-1/2-inch **LIGHT GOLD** square. Draw a diagonal line on the squares; stitch, trim, and press.

Make 1

Step 2 Sew 2-1/2 x 4-1/2-inch **BLUE** rectangles to both side edges of the Step 1 unit; press. With right sides together, position 2-1/2-inch **LIGHT GOLD** squares on the corners of a 2-1/2 x 8-1/2-inch **BLUE** rectangle. Draw a diagonal line on the squares; stitch, trim, and press. Sew the units to the top/bottom edges of the unit; press. <u>At this point the unit should measure 8-1/2-inches square.</u>

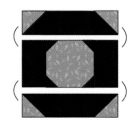

Make 2

Make 1

Step 3 With right sides together, position a 2-1/2-inch **GOLD FLORAL** square on the corner of a 2-1/2 x 4-1/2-inch **RED #3** rectangle. Draw a

diagonal line on the square; stitch, trim, and press. Repeat this process on the opposite corner of the rectangle.

Make 4

Step 4 With right sides together, position a 2-1/2-inch **BEIGE** square on the corner of a 2-1/2 x 4-1/2-inch **GOLD FLORAL** rectangle. Draw a diagonal line on the square; stitch, trim; press. Repeat this process on the opposite corner of the rectangle. Make 4 units. Sew the units to the top edge of the Step 3 units; press.

Make 4

( )

Make 4

Step 5 With right sides together, position a 2-1/2-inch **BEIGE** square on the corner of a 2-1/2 x 4-1/2-inch **RED #3** rectangle. Draw a diagonal line on the square; stitch, trim, and press. Make 4 units. Referring to the diagram, reverse the direction of the stitching line to make 4 more units. Sew the units to both side edges of the Step 4 units; press. <u>At this point the units should measure 4-1/2 x 8-1/2-inches.</u>

Make 4   *Make 4*

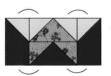

Make 4

Step 6 With right sides together, layer the 2-7/8-inch **BEIGE** and **RED #3** squares in pairs. Press together, but do not sew. Cut the layered squares in half diagonally to make 4 sets of triangles. Stitch

1/4-inch from the diagonal edge of each pair of triangles; press. Referring to the diagram for placement, sew the triangle-pieced squares and 2-1/2-inch **GOLD FLORAL** squares together in pairs; press. Sew the remaining 2-1/2-inch **GOLD FLORAL** and **RED #3** squares together in pairs; press. Sew the units together; press. <u>At this point each unit should measure 4-1/2-inches square.</u>

Make 4

Make 4 *Make 4* *Make 4*

Step 7 Sew the Step 5 units to both side edges of the Step 2 unit; press. Sew the Step 6 units to both side edges of the remaining Step 5 units; press. Referring to the block assembly diagram, sew the units together; press. <u>At this point the block should measure 16-1/2-inches square.</u>

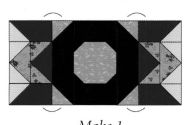
Make 1

Make 2

Make 1

Step 8 Referring to the quilt center diagram, sew the shoo fly blocks to the woodland flower block; press. <u>At this point the unit should measure 24-1/2-inches square.</u>

Quilt Center

Referring to the quilt center diagram for placement, sew the units together; press. <u>At this point the quilt center should measure 42-1/2 x 48-1/2-inches.</u>

Quilt Center Diagram

Borders

*Note: The yardage given allows for the border strips to be cut on the crosswise grain. Diagonally piece the strips as needed, referring to **Diagonal Piecing** on page 159 for complete instructions. Read through **Border** instructions on page 158 for general instructions on adding borders.*

Cutting

From **CHESTNUT PRINT**:
- Cut 5, 2-1/2 x 42-inch inner border strips

From **BLACK PRINT #2**:
- Cut 7, 6-1/2 x 42-inch outer border strips

Attaching the Borders

Step 1 Attach the 2-1/2-inch wide **CHESTNUT** inner border strips.

Step 2 Attach the 6-1/2-inch wide **BLACK #2** outer border strips.

Putting It All Together

Cut the 3-3/4 yard length of backing fabric in half crosswise to make 2, 1-7/8 yard lengths. Refer to ***Finishing the Quilt*** on page 159 for complete instructions.

Binding

Cutting

From **MULTICOLOR PLAID**:
- Cut enough 2-3/4-inch wide **bias** strips to make a 260-inch long strip.

Sew the binding to the quilt using a 3/8-inch seam allowance. This measurement will produce a 1/2-inch wide finished double binding. Refer to ***Binding*** and ***Diagonal Piecing*** on page 159 for complete instructions.

Nature Walk Wallhanging

58 x 64-inches

*Triangle blocks in jewel tones work up quickly to
create festive Christmas patches
that are sure to brighten any holiday table.*

Christmas Patches

Tablecloth

74-inches square

Fabrics and Supplies

25 fat quarters of **ASSORTED MEDIUM** to **DARK PRINTS** for triangle blocks

1/2 yard **BLACK PRINT** for inner border

1/2 yard **GOLD PRINT** for middle border

1-1/3 yards **RED PRINT** for outer border

3/4 yard **BLACK PRINT** for binding

4-1/2 yards for backing

quilt batting, at least 82-inches square

Triangle Blocks

Makes 100 blocks

Cutting

From each of the **ASSORTED MEDIUM** to **DARK PRINTS:**

- Cut 4, 7-1/4-inch squares. Cut the squares diagonally into quarters to make 16 triangles from each print (a total of 400 triangles).

Piecing

Step 1 With right sides together, layer the triangles together in pairs. Stitch along the same bias edge of each set of layered triangles being careful not to stretch the triangles; press.

Bias edges

Make 200 triangle sets

Step 2 Sew the triangle sets together in pairs to make the triangle blocks; press. <u>At this point each triangle block should measure 6-1/2-inches square.</u>

Make 100 triangle blocks

Quilt Center

Step 1 Referring to the quilt diagram for placement, sew the triangle blocks together in 10 rows of 10 blocks each. Press the seam allowances in alternating directions by rows so the seams will fit snugly together with less bulk.

Step 2 Pin the rows at the block intersections; sew the rows together. Press the seam allowances in one direction. At this point the quilt center should measure 60-1/2-inches square.

Borders

*Note: The yardage given allows for the border strips to be cut on the crosswise grain. Diagonally piece the strips as needed, referring to **Diagonal Piecing** instructions on page 159. Read through **Border** instructions on page 158 for general instructions on adding borders.*

Cutting

From **BLACK PRINT:**
- Cut 7, 1-1/2 x 42-inch inner border strips

From **GOLD PRINT:**
- Cut 7, 1-1/2 x 42-inch middle border strips

From **RED PRINT:**
- Cut 8, 5-1/2 x 42-inch outer border strips

Attaching the Borders

Step 1 Attach the 1-1/2-inch wide **BLACK** inner border strips.

Step 2 Attach the 1-1/2-inch wide **GOLD** middle border strips.

Step 3 Attach the 5-1/2 -inch wide **RED** outer border strips.

Putting It All Together

Cut the 4-1/2 yard length of backing fabric in half crosswise to make 2, 2-1/4 yard lengths. Refer to *Finishing the Quilt* on page 159 for complete instructions.

Binding

From **BLACK PRINT:**
- Cut 8, 2-3/4 x 42-inch strips

Sew the binding to the quilt using a 3/8-inch seam allowance. This measurement will produce a 1/2-inch wide finished double binding. Refer to *Binding* and *Diagonal Piecing* instructions on page 159 for complete instructions.

Christmas Patches Tablecloth

74-inches square

*Christmas bloom appliqués blend beautifully with
holiday-themed decorating and the soft yellow, beige and gold prints
offer a refreshing change from the traditional red, white and green.*

Christmas Bloom

Wallhanging

44-inches square

Fabrics and Supplies

1/4 yard **YELLOW PRINT** for pieced blocks

7/8 yard **BEIGE PRINT** for pieced blocks, checkerboard and block border

3/8 yard **GOLD PRINT** for block borders and middle border

5/8 yard **GREEN PRINT** for checkerboard, corner squares, inner border, flower center, leaf, and stem appliqués

1-1/8 yards **RED FLORAL** for checkerboard, corner squares, outer border, and flower petal appliqués

5/8 yard **TAN/ROSE FLORAL** for side and corner triangles

1/2 yard **YELLOW PRINT** for binding

2-3/4 yards for backing

quilt batting, at least 50-inches square

paper-backed fusible web

pearl cotton or embroidery floss for decorative stitches: black, gold, red

Blocks

Makes 5 blocks

Cutting

From **BEIGE PRINT:**
- Cut 1, 3-1/2 x 20-inch strip. From the strip cut: 5, 3-1/2-inch squares
- Cut 10, 1-1/2 x 42-inch strips
- Cut 4, 1 x 42-inch block border strips

From **YELLOW PRINT:**
- Cut 4, 1-1/2 x 42-inch strips

From **GOLD PRINT:**
- Cut 4, 1 x 42-inch block border strips

From **GREEN PRINT:**
- Cut 4, 2-1/2-inch corner squares
- Cut 5, 1-1/2 x 42-inch strips

From **RED FLORAL:**
- Cut 1, 2-1/2 x 42-inch strip. From the strip cut: 16, 2-1/2-inch corner squares
- Cut 1, 1-1/2 x 42-inch strip

Piecing the Block Center

Step 1 Align long edges, sew 1-1/2 x 42-inch **BEIGE** strips to both side edges of a 1-1/2 x 42-inch **YELLOW** strip. Press the seam allowances toward the **YELLOW** strip. Cut the strip set into segments.

Crosscut 10, 1-1/2-inch wide segments

Step 2   Sew Step 1 segments to the top/bottom edges of the 3-1/2-inch **BEIGE** squares; press.

Make 5

Step 3   Aligning long edges, sew together 3 of the 1-1/2 x 42-inch **YELLOW** strips and 2 of the 1-1/2 x 42-inch **BEIGE** strips. Press the seam allowances toward the **YELLOW** strips. Cut the strip set into segments.

Crosscut 10, 1-1/2-inch wide segments

Step 4   Sew the Step 3 segments to the side edges of the Step 2 units; press. <u>At this point each block center should measure 5-1/2-inches square.</u>

Make 5

Step 5   To attach the 1-inch wide **BEIGE** border strips to each block, refer to ***Border*** instructions on page 158.

Step 6   To attach the 1-inch wide **GOLD** border strips to each block, refer to ***Border*** instructions. <u>At this point each block center should measure 7-1/2-inches square.</u>

Make 5

Fusible Web Appliqué Method

The appliqué shapes are on page 126. The decorative stitch diagrams are on page 158.

Step 1   Trace 15 flower petals, 5 flower centers, 5 leaves, and 5 stems on the paper side of the fusible web, leaving 1/2-inch between each shape. Cut the shapes apart, leaving a small margin beyond the drawn lines.

Step 2   Following the manufacturer's instructions, fuse the shapes to the wrong side of the fabrics chosen for the appliqués. Let the fabric cool; cut on the traced line. Peel away the paper backing from the fusible web.

Step 3   Referring to the block diagram below, position the appliqué shapes on the pieced block center; fuse in place. Blanket stitch around the leaf/stem/flower center shapes with black pearl cotton or 3 strands of embroidery floss. Use gold pearl cotton/embroidery thread to blanket stitch around the flower petals. Stitch 3 French knots above the flower centers with red pearl cotton/embroidery floss.

Note: *To prevent the blanket stitches from "rolling off" the edges of the appliqué shapes, take an extra backstitch in the same place as you made the blanket stitch, going around outer curves, corners, and points. For straight edges, taking a backstitch every inch is enough.*

Make 5

Piecing the Block Borders

Step 1   Aligning long edges, sew together a 1-1/2 x 42-inch **GREEN** and **BEIGE** strip. Press the seam allowance toward the **GREEN** strip. Make a total of 5 strip sets. Cut the strip sets into segments.

Crosscut 112,
1-1/2-inch wide segments

Step 2   Sew together 7 of the segments to make a checkerboard unit; press.

Make 16

Step 3   Sew checkerboard units to the top/bottom edges of 4 appliquéd blocks; press. Sew 2-1/2-inch **RED FLORAL** corner squares to both ends of the remaining **GREEN/BEIGE** checkerboard units; press. Sew the units to the side edges of the appliquéd blocks; press. At this point each block should measure 11-1/2-inches square.

Make 4

Step 4   Aligning long edges, sew together a 1-1/2 x 42-inch **RED FLORAL** and **BEIGE** strip. Press the seam allowance toward the **RED FLORAL** strip. Cut the strip set into segments.

Crosscut 28, 1-1/2-inch wide segments

Step 5   Sew together 7 of the segments to make a checkerboard unit; press.

Make 4

Step 6   Sew a checkerboard unit to the top/bottom edges of the remaining appliquéd block; press. Sew 2-1/2-inch **GREEN** corner squares to both ends of the remaining **RED FLORAL/BEIGE**

checkerboard units; press. Sew the units to the side edges of the appliquéd block; press. At this point the block should measure 11-1/2-inches square.

Make 1

Quilt Center

Note: *The side and corner triangles are larger than necessary and will be trimmed before the borders are added.*

Cutting

From **TAN/ROSE FLORAL:**

• Cut 1, 18 x 42-inch strip. From the strip cut:
1, 18-inch square. Cut the square diagonally into quarters to make 4 side triangles.
2, 9-inch squares. Cut the squares in half diagonally to make 4 corner triangles.

Quilt Center Assembly

Step 1   Referring to the quilt diagram for placement, sew together the blocks and the side triangles in diagonal rows. Press the seam allowances in alternating directions by rows so the seams will fit snugly together with less bulk.

Step 2   Pin the rows together at the block intersections; sew the rows together and press.

Step 3   Sew the corner triangles to the quilt center; press.

Step 4   Trim away the excess fabric from the side and corner triangles, taking care to allow a 1/4-inch seam allowance beyond the corners of each block. Refer to ***Trimming Side and Corner Triangles*** on page 126.

Trimming Side and Corner Triangles

Begin at a corner by lining up your ruler 1/4-inch beyond the points of the corners of the blocks as shown. Cut along the edge of the ruler. Repeat this procedure on all four sides of the quilt top.

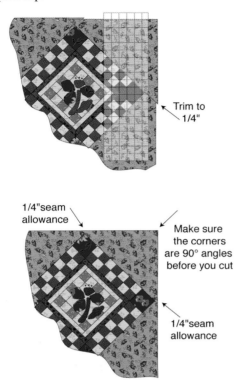

Step 2 Attach the 1-inch wide **GOLD** middle border strips.

Step 3 Attach the 5-1/2-inch wide **RED FLORAL** outer border strips.

Putting It All Together

Cut the 2-3/4 yard length of backing fabric in half crosswise to make 2, 1-3/8 yard lengths. Refer to *Finishing the Quilt* on page 159 for complete instructions.

Binding

Cutting

From **YELLOW PRINT:**
- Cut 5, 2-3/4 x 42-inch strips

Sew the binding to the quilt using a 3/8-inch seam allowance. This measurement will produce a 1/2-inch wide finished double binding. Refer to *Binding* and *Diagonal Piecing* instructions on page 159 for complete instructions.

Borders

Note: *The yardage given allows for the border strips to be cut on the crosswise grain. Diagonally piece the strips as needed, referring to **Diagonal Piecing** instructions on page 159. Read through **Border** instructions on page 158 for general instructions on adding borders.*

Cutting

From **GREEN PRINT:**
- Cut 4, 1-1/2 x 42-inch inner border strips

From **GOLD PRINT:**
- Cut 4, 1 x 42-inch middle border strips

From **RED FLORAL:**
- Cut 5, 5-1/2 x 42-inch outer border strips

Attaching the Borders

Step 1 Attach the 1-1/2-inch wide **GREEN** inner border strips.

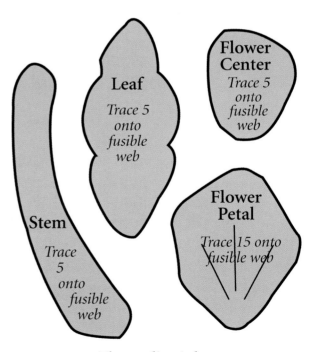

The appliqué shapes are reversed for tracing purposes.

Christmas Bloom Wallhanging

44-inches square

From the coiled rug on the floor to the flea market finds surrounding the Sunshine Porch quilt, the mood is an invitation to relax. The nightstand is a vintage kitchen stool with steps that pull out to store bedtime reading.

Sunshine Porch

Quilt

75 x 92-inches

Fabrics and Supplies

1-1/2 yards **BEIGE PRINT**
for block background

1 yard **YELLOW PRINT** for blocks

1 yard **BLUE PRINT**
for blocks and middle border

2/3 yard **GREEN PRINT** for blocks

3-7/8 yards **RED TOILE**
for alternate blocks, inner and outer borders

1-5/8 yards **RED PRINT**
for side and corner triangles

1-7/8 yards **BLUE PRINT** for binding

5-1/2 yards for backing

quilt batting, at least 81 x 98-inches

Pieced Blocks

Makes 12 blocks

Cutting

From **BEIGE PRINT**:

- Cut 4, 2-7/8 x 42-inch strips. From the strips cut:
  48, 2-7/8-inch squares. Cut the squares in half diagonally to make 96 triangles.
- Cut 12, 2-1/2 x 42-inch strips. From the strips cut:
  48, 2-1/2 x 4-1/2-inch rectangles
  96, 2-1/2-inch squares

From **YELLOW PRINT**:

- Cut 9, 2-1/2 x 42-inch strips. From the strips cut:
  48, 2-1/2 x 4-1/2-inch rectangles
  48, 2-1/2-inch squares

From **BLUE PRINT**:

- Cut 2, 4-1/2 x 42-inch strips. From the strips cut:
  12, 4-1/2-inch squares

From **GREEN PRINT**:

- Cut 3, 4-7/8 x 42-inch strips. From the strips cut:
  24, 4-7/8-inch squares. Cut the squares in half diagonally to make 48 triangles.

Piecing

Step 1 With right sides together, position a 2-1/2-inch **BEIGE** square on the corner of a 2-1/2 x 4-1/2-inch **YELLOW** rectangle. Draw a diagonal line on the square and stitch on the line. Trim the seam allowance to 1/4-inch; press. Repeat this process at the opposite corner of the rectangle. Sew a 2-1/2 x 4-1/2-inch

BEIGE rectangle to the top edge of the unit; press. <u>At this point each unit should measure 4-1/2-inches square.</u>

Make 48   *Make 48*

Step 2 Sew a **BEIGE** triangle to the edge of a 2-1/2-inch **YELLOW** square; press. Sew another **BEIGE** triangle to the adjacent edge of the square; press. Sew this unit to the bias edge of a **GREEN** triangle; press. <u>At this point each unit should measure 4-1/2-inches square.</u>

Make 48

Step 3 Sew the Step 2 units to both side edges of 24 of the Step 1 units; press. <u>At this point each section should measure 4-1/2 x 12-1/2-inches.</u>

Make 24

Step 4 Sew the remaining Step 1 units to both side edges of the 4-1/2-inch **BLUE** squares; press. <u>At this point each section should measure 4-1/2 x 12-1/2-inches.</u>

Make 12

Step 5 Sew the Step 3 sections to the top/bottom edges of the Step 4 sections; press. <u>At this point each block should measure 12-1/2-inches square.</u>

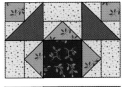

Make 12

Quilt Center

Note: *The side and corner triangles are larger than necessary and will be trimmed before the borders are added.*

Cutting

From **RED TOILE**:

- Cut 2, 12-1/2 x 42-inch strips. From the strips cut: 6, 12-1/2-inch squares for alternate blocks.

From **RED PRINT**:

- Cut 2, 19-1/2 x 42-inch strips. From the strips cut: 3, 19-1/2-inch squares. Cut the squares diagonally into quarters to make 12 triangles. You will be using only 10 for side triangles.

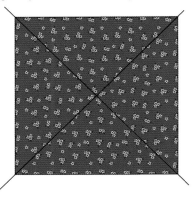

- Cut 1, 11 x 42-inch strip. From the strip cut: 2, 11-inch squares. Cut the squares in half diagonally to make 4 corner triangles.

Quilt Center Assembly

Step 1 Referring to the quilt center assembly diagram for block placement, sew together the pieced blocks, 12-1/2-inch square **RED TOILE** alternate blocks, and **RED** side triangles. Press the seam allowances away from the pieced blocks.

Quilt Center Assembly Diagram

Step 2 Pin the rows together at the block intersections; stitch together and press.

Step 3 Sew the **RED** corner triangles to the quilt center; press.

Step 4 Trim away the excess fabric from the side and corner triangles taking care to allow a 1/4-inch seam allowance beyond the corners of each block. Refer to *Trimming Side and Corner Triangles* at right.

Trimming Side and Corner Triangles

Begin at a corner by lining up your ruler 1/4-inch beyond the points of the corners of the blocks as shown. Cut along the edge of the ruler. Repeat this procedure on all four sides of the quilt top.

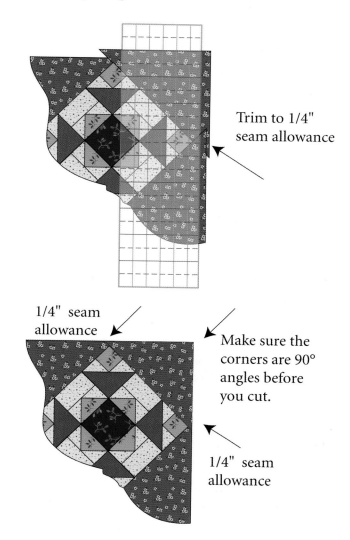

Trim to 1/4" seam allowance

1/4" seam allowance

Make sure the corners are 90° angles before you cut.

1/4" seam allowance

Borders

Note: *The yardage given allows for the border strips to be cut on the crosswise grain. Diagonally piece the strips as needed, referring to* **Diagonal Piecing** *instructions on page 159. Read through* **Border** *instructions on page 158 for general instructions on adding borders.*

Cutting

From **RED TOILE:**

- Cut 10, 8-1/2 x 42-inch outer border strips
- Cut 7, 2-1/2 x 42-inch inner border strips

From **BLUE PRINT:**

- Cut 7, 2-1/2 x 42-inch middle border strips

Attaching the Borders

Step 1 Attach the 2-1/2-inch wide **RED TOILE** inner border strips.

Step 2 Attach the 2-1/2-inch wide **BLUE** middle border strips.

Step 3 Attach the 8-1/2-inch wide **RED TOILE** outer border strips.

Putting It All Together

Cut the 5-1/2 yard length of backing fabric in half crosswise to make 2, 2-3/4 yard lengths. Refer to **Finishing the Quilt** on page 159 for complete instructions.

Binding

Cutting

From **BLUE PRINT:**

- Cut 9, 6-1/2 x 42-inch strips

Sew the binding to the quilt using a scant 1-inch seam allowance. This measurement will produce a 1-inch wide finished double binding. Refer to **Binding** and **Diagonal Piecing** on page 159 for complete instructions.

Quilting Suggestions:

- Red Toile alternate blocks - TB10 Radish Top.
- Pieced Blocks - in the ditch.
- Red side triangles - TB40-12" Corner Swirl.
- Red corner triangles - TB40-9" Corner Swirl.
- The three borders quilted as one - large meander.

The **THIMBLEBERRIES**® *quilt stencils are by Quilting Creations International.*

TB10 Radish Top Quilting Suggestion

TB40 Corner Swirl Quilting Suggestion

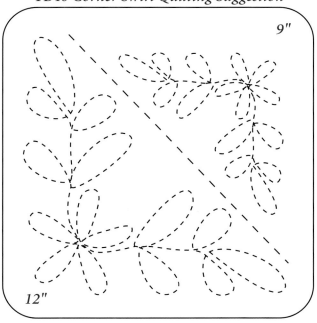

Sunshine Porch Quilt

75 x 92-inches

Guests will question whether your Puzzle Perfect throw was designed with pinwheel or diamond blocks. They'll never guess it's a combination of both designs in one creative block.

Puzzle Perfect

Throw

48-inches square

Fabrics and Supplies

3/4 yard **GREEN PRINT**
for blocks and pieced border

3/4 yard **BLUE PRINT**
for blocks and pieced border

1/2 yard **BEIGE PRINT** for background

1-1/4 yards **LARGE RED FLORAL**
for blocks, corner squares, and pieced border

1/2 yard **CHESTNUT PRINT**
for inner border and pieced border

1/2 yard **CHESTNUT PRINT** for binding

3 yards for backing

quilt batting, at least 54-inches square

Pieced Blocks

Makes 9 blocks

Cutting

From GREEN PRINT:
- Cut 2, 3-1/2 x 42-inch strips. From the strips cut: 18, 3-1/2-inch squares
- Cut 1, 7-1/4 x 42-inch strip. From the strip cut: 5, 7-1/4-inch squares. Cut the squares diagonally into quarters to make 20 triangles. You will be using only 18 triangles.

From BLUE PRINT:
- Cut 2, 3-1/2 x 42-inch strips. From the strips cut: 18, 3-1/2-inch squares
- Cut 1, 7-1/4 x 42-inch strip. From the strip cut: 5, 7-1/4-inch squares. Cut the squares diagonally into quarters to make 20 triangles. You will be using only 18 triangles.

From BEIGE PRINT:
- Cut 2, 7-1/4 x 42-inch strips. From the strips cut: 9, 7-1/4-inch squares. Cut the squares diagonally into quarters to make 36 triangles.

From LARGE RED FLORAL:
- Cut 4, 6-7/8 x 42-inch strips. From the strips cut: 18, 6-7/8-inch squares. Cut the squares in half diagonally to make 36 triangles.

Piecing

Step 1 With right sides together, layer a **GREEN** triangle on a **BEIGE** triangle. Stitch along 1 bias edge; press. Repeat this process to make 18 sets of triangles, stitching along the same bias edge of each triangle set.

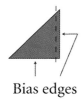

Bias edges   *Make 18*

Step 2 Sew together the Step 1 triangle sets and 18 **LARGE RED FLORAL** triangles. Press the seam allowances toward the **LARGE RED FLORAL** triangles. Position a 3-1/2-inch **BLUE** square on the corner of the **LARGE RED FLORAL** triangle. Draw a diagonal line on the square and stitch on the line. Trim the seam allowance to 1/4-inch. Press the seam allowance toward the **LARGE RED FLORAL** triangle. <u>At this point each unit should measure 6-1/2-inches square.</u>

Make 18

Step 3 With right sides together, layer a **BLUE** triangle on a **BEIGE** triangle. Stitch along 1 bias edge; press. Repeat this process to make 18 sets of triangles, stitching along the same bias edge of each triangle set.

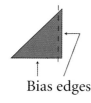

Bias edges

Step 4 Sew together the Step 3 triangle sets and 18 **LARGE RED FLORAL** triangles. Press the seam allowances toward the **LARGE RED FLORAL** triangles. Position a 3-1/2-inch **GREEN** square on the corner of the **LARGE RED FLORAL** triangle.

Draw a diagonal line on the square; stitch, trim, and press. <u>At this point each unit should measure 6-1/2-inches square.</u>

Make 18

Step 5 Referring to the block diagram for placement, sew together the Step 2 and Step 3 units in pairs; press. Sew the pairs together; press. <u>At this point each pieced block should measure 12-1/2-inches square.</u>

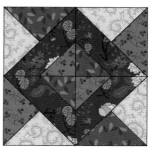

Make 9

Step 6 Referring to the quilt diagram, sew the blocks together in 3 rows with 3 blocks in each row. Press the seam allowances in alternating directions by rows so the seams will fit snugly together with less bulk.

Step 7 Pin the rows together at the block intersections; sew together and press.

Borders

***Note:** The yardage given allows for the border strips to be cut on the crosswise grain. Diagonally piece the strips as needed, referring to **Diagonal Piecing** instructions on page 159. Read through **Border** instructions on page 158 for general instructions on adding borders.*

Cutting

From **GREEN PRINT:**
- Cut 3, 2-1/2 x 42-inch strips for pieced border

From **BLUE PRINT:**
- Cut 3, 2-1/2 x 42-inch strips for pieced border

From **LARGE RED FLORAL:**
- Cut 3, 2-1/2 x 42-inch strips for pieced border
- Cut 1, 4-1/2 x 42-inch strip. From the strip cut:
  4, 4-1/2-inch larger corner squares
  4, 2-1/2-inch smaller corner squares

From **CHESTNUT PRINT:**
- Cut 5, 2-1/2 x 42-inch strips. From the strips cut:
  4, 2-1/2 x 36-1/2-inch inner border strips
  8, 2-1/2 x 4-1/2-inch rectangles for pieced border

Assembling and Attaching the Borders

Step 1 Attach the 2-1/2-inch wide **CHESTNUT** top/bottom inner border strips.

Step 2 For the side borders, measure the quilt center from top to bottom through the middle including the seam allowances, but not the borders just added. Cut 2 of the 2-1/2-inch wide **CHESTNUT** side border strips to this length. Sew the 2-1/2-inch **LARGE RED FLORAL** small corner squares to both ends of the **CHESTNUT** side border strips; press. Sew the border strips to the side edges of the quilt center; press.

Step 3 Aligning long edges, sew together 1 of each of the 2-1/2 x 42-inch **GREEN, LARGE RED FLORAL,** and **BLUE** strips. Press referring to *Hints and Helps for Pressing Strip Sets* on page 158. Make 3 strip sets. Cut the strip sets into segments.

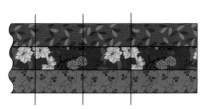

Crosscut 24,
4-1/2-inch wide segments

Step 4 For each pieced border, sew together 6 of the Step 3 segments; press. Sew 2-1/2 x 4-1/2-inch **CHESTNUT** rectangles to both ends of each piece border strip; press.

Make 4

Step 5 Sew pieced border strips to the top/bottom edges of the quilt center; press.

Step 6 Sew 4-1/2-inch **RED** large corner squares to both ends of the remaining pieced border strips; press. Sew the pieced border strips to the side edges of the quilt center; press.

Putting It All Together

Cut the 3 yard length of backing fabric in half crosswise to make 2, 1-1/2 yard lengths. Refer to *Finishing the Quilt* on page 159 for complete instructions.

Binding

Cutting

From **CHESTNUT PRINT:**
- Cut 5, 2-3/4 x 42-inch strips

Sew the binding to the quilt using a 3/8-inch seam allowance. This measurement will produce a 1/2-inch wide finished double binding. Refer to *Binding* and *Diagonal Piecing* on page 159 for complete instructions.

Quilting Suggestions:

- Pieced blocks - TB14 Bur Oak.
- Chestnut inner border - TB30 Beadwork.
- Pieced border - in the ditch.

The diagrams of the quilt stencils are on page 139.

*The **THIMBLEBERRIES**® quilt stencils are by Quilting Creations International.*

*Create an eye-catching corner by adorning a grapevine
wreath with a bright throw. A wooden picket fence embellished
with tin pine tree and star round out the display.*

TB14 Bur Oak Quilting Suggestion

TB30 Beadwork Quilting Suggestion

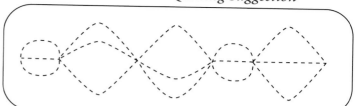

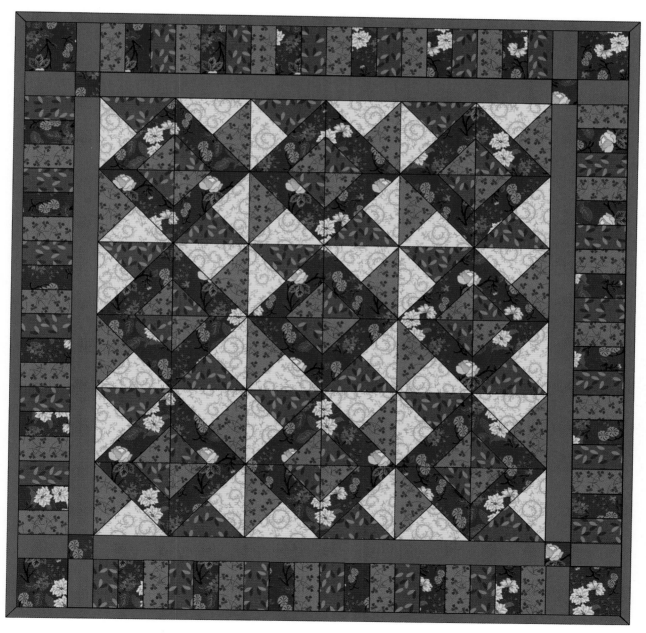

Puzzle Perfect Throw

48-inches square

Romantic roses on a ruffled pillow sham are reminiscent of days gone by when even suitcases were made to last a lifetime. Here, a child's chair holds a vintage suitcase which is collectible as well as functional for small space decorating.

Ruffled Pillow Sham

Pillow Sham

20 x 26-inches

Fabrics and Supplies

2-1/8 yards **LARGE ROSE FLORAL**
(nondirectional)
for center rectangle, pillow top bands,
ruffles, and pillow backing

1/3 yard **BEIGE PRINT** for pillow top bands

20 x 26-inch bed pillow

Pillow Top

Cutting

From **LARGE ROSE FLORAL:**
- Cut 1, 9-1/2 x 42-inch strip. From the strip cut:
  1, 9-1/2 x 20-1/2-inch center rectangle
  2, 2 x 20-1/2-inch bands

From **BEIGE PRINT:**
- Cut 1, 4-1/8 x 42-inch strip. From the strip cut:
  2, 4-1/8 x 20-1/2-inch bands
- Cut 2, 2-3/8 x 42-inch strips. From the strips cut:
  4, 2-3/8 x 20-1/2-inch bands

Piecing

Step 1 Referring to the diagram below, sew 2 of the
2-3/8 x 20-1/2-inch **BEIGE** bands to both
side edges of the 9-1/2 x 20-1/2-inch **LARGE
ROSE FLORAL** center rectangle; press.

Step 1
Make 1 center unit

Step 2 Sew together a 2-3/8 x 20-1/2-inch **BEIGE** band, a 2 x 20-1/2-inch **LARGE ROSE FLORAL** band, and a 4-1/8 x 20-1/2-inch **BEIGE** band; press.

Step 2
Make 2 side units

Ruffles

Cutting

From LARGE ROSE FLORAL:

- Cut 2, 6-1/2 x 40-inch strips for outer edge larger ruffles
- Cut 2, 4-1/2 x 40-inch strips for smaller ruffles

Attaching the Ruffles

Step 1 Fold a 4-1/2-inch wide **LARGE ROSE FLORAL** strip in half lengthwise, wrong sides together; press. Divide the ruffle strip into 4 equal segments; mark the quarter points with safety pins.

Step 2 To gather the ruffle, position a heavy thread 1/4-inch in from the raw edges of the ruffle strip. You will need a length of thread 40-inches long. Secure 1 end of the thread by stitching across it. Zigzag stitch over the thread the length of the strip, taking care not to sew through it. Repeat with the remaining 4-1/2-inch wide strip.

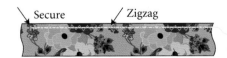

Secure   Zigzag

Step 3 Divide the right side edge of the Step 1 center unit into 4 equal segments; mark the quarter points with safety pins. With right sides together and raw edges aligned, pin a prepared smaller

ruffle to the right edge of the Step 1 center unit; matching the quarter points. Pull up the gathering stitches until the ruffle fits the pillow front. Machine baste the ruffle in place using a scant 1/4-inch seam allowance. Repeat this process to attach the remaining smaller ruffle to the left edge of the center unit.

Step 4 With right sides together, layer a Step 2 side unit on the right edge of the center unit; pin. The ruffle will be sandwiched between the 2 layers and turned in toward the center of the pillow at this time. Pin and stitch the units together using a 3/8-inch seam allowance. Repeat this process to attach the remaining side unit to the left edge of the center unit.

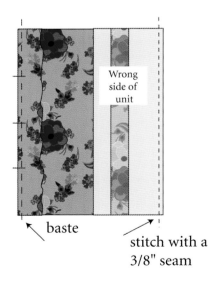

Wrong side of unit

baste

stitch with a 3/8" seam

Step 5 Press the seam allowances toward the center unit so the ruffles will be going away from the center unit. Machine baste the top and bottom raw edges of the ruffles to the pillow top. <u>At this point the pillow top should measure 20-1/2 x 26-3/4-inches.</u>

↓ Baste ruffles in place ↓

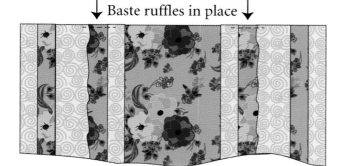

Step 6 The short ends of the larger ruffles need to be finished before the 6-1/2-inch wide **LARGE ROSE FLORAL** strips are made into ruffles. To do this, with right sides together, fold a 6-1/2-inch wide strip in half. Stitch across each end, clip the corners, and turn the ends right side out. With wrong sides together, fold the entire strip in half lengthwise; press. Divide the ruffle into 4 equal segments; mark the quarter points. Gather the ruffle as instructed in Step 2. Repeat with the remaining 6-1/2-inch wide strip.

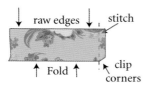

raw edges   stitch

Fold   clip corners

Step 7 The ends of the larger ruffles need to be set back 3/8-inch from the top/bottom edges of the pillow top so they won't get caught in the seam allowance. Divide the side edges of the pillow top into 4 equal segments; mark the quarter points. With right sides together and raw edges aligned, pin the prepared larger ruffles to the pillow top. Pull up the gathering stitches until the ruffle fits the pillow top. Machine baste the ruffle in place.

set back 3/8" away from edge

Baste

Pillow Back

Cutting

From **LARGE ROSE FLORAL:**

• Cut 2, 20-1/2 x 36-inch pillow back rectangles

Assembling the Pillow Back

Step 1 With wrong sides together, fold each 20-1/2 x 36-inch **LARGE ROSE FLORAL** pillow rectangle in half crosswise to make 2, 18 x 20-1/2-inch double-thick pillow back pieces. Overlap the 2 folded edges so the pillow back measures 20-1/2 x 26-1/2-inches. Pin the pieces together and stitch around the entire piece to create a single pillow back; using a scant 1/4-inch seam allowance. The double thickness of each back piece will make the pillow back more stable. This technique will give your pillow back a nice finishing touch.

Overlap

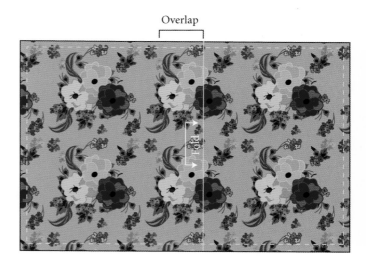

Step 2 With wrong sides together, layer the pillow back and the pillow front; pin. The outer ruffles will be sandwiched between the 2 layers and turned in toward the center of the pillow at this time. Pin and stitch around the outside edges using a 3/8-inch seam allowance.

Step 3 Turn the pillow right side out, insert the pillow form through the pillow back opening; fluff up the ruffle.

A churn used in making butter inspired the block that is as popular today as it was in yesteryear. Twelve big blocks surrounded by a checkerboard border make this quilt a Churn Dash Delight.

Churn Dash Delight

Quilt

76 x 90-inches

Fabrics and Supplies

2/3 yard **GREEN FLORAL**
for blocks and lattice posts

3-5/8 yards **PURPLE FLORAL**
for blocks and outer border

3/4 yard **BEIGE PRINT #1**
for block backgrounds

7/8 yard **BEIGE PRINT #2**
for block backgrounds

1/2 yard **GOLD PRINT**
for lattice segments

3/4 yard **GREEN PRINT**
for inner border and checkerboard border

1-1/3 yards **GREEN DIAGONAL CHECK**
for middle border
and checkerboard border

7/8 yard **GREEN PRINT** for binding

5-1/3 yards for backing

quilt batting, at least 82 x 96-inches

Block A

Makes 6 blocks

Cutting

From **BEIGE PRINT #1:**
- Cut 2, 4-7/8 x 42-inch strips
- Cut 1, 4-1/2 x 42-inch strip. From the strip cut: 6, 4-1/2-inch squares
- Cut 3, 2-1/2 x 42-inch strips

From **GREEN FLORAL:**
- Cut 2, 4-7/8 x 42-inch strips

From **PURPLE FLORAL:**
- Cut 3, 2-1/2 x 42-inch strips

Piecing

Step 1 With right sides together, layer the 4-7/8 x 42-inch **GREEN FLORAL** and **BEIGE #1** strips together in pairs. Press together, but do not sew. Cut the layered strips into squares. Cut the layered squares in half diagonally to make 24 sets of triangles. Stitch 1/4-inch from the diagonal edge of each pair of triangles; press.

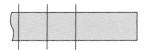

Crosscut 12, 4-7/8-inch squares

Make 24, 4-1/2-inch triangle-pieced squares

Step 2 Aligning long edges, sew the 2-1/2 x 42-inch **BEIGE #1** and **PURPLE FLORAL** strips together in pairs. Press referring to *Hints and Helps for Pressing Strip Sets* on page 158. Make a total of 3 strip sets. Cut the strip sets into squares.

Crosscut 24, 4-7/8-inch squares

Step 3 Referring to the diagram for placement, sew Step 1 triangle-pieced squares to both side edges of a Step 2 square; press. At this point each A Unit should measure 4-1/2 x 12-1/2-inches.

A Unit
Make 12

Step 4 Sew Step 2 squares to both side edges of a 4-1/2-inch **BEIGE #1** square; press. At this point each B Unit should measure 4-1/2 x 12-1/2-inches.

B Unit
Make 6

Step 5 Sew A Units to the top/bottom edges of a B Unit; press. At this point each Block A should measure 12-1/2-inches square.

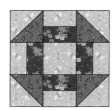

Block A
Make 6

Block B

Makes 6 blocks

Cutting

From **BEIGE PRINT #2:**
- Cut 2, 4-7/8 x 42-inch strips
- Cut 1, 4-1/2 x 42-inch strip. From the strip cut: 6, 4-1/2-inch squares
- Cut 3, 2-1/2 x 42-inch strips

From **PURPLE FLORAL:**
- Cut 2, 4-7/8 x 42-inch strips

From **GREEN FLORAL:**
- Cut 3, 2-1/2 x 42-inch strips

Piecing

Step 1 With right sides together, layer the 4-7/8 x 42-inch **PURPLE FLORAL** and **BEIGE #2** strips together in pairs. Press together, but do not sew. Cut the layered strips into squares. Cut the layered squares in half diagonally to make 24 sets of triangles. Stitch 1/4-inch from the diagonal edge of each pair of triangles; press.

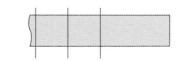

Crosscut 12, 4-7/8-inch squares

Make 24, 4-1/2-inch triangle-pieced squares

Step 2 Aligning long edges, sew the 2-1/2 x 42-inch **BEIGE #2** and **GREEN FLORAL** strips together in pairs; press. Make a total of 3 strip sets. Cut the strip sets into squares.

Crosscut 24, 4-1/2-inch squares

Step 3 Referring to the diagram for placement, sew Step 1 triangle-pieced squares to both side edges of a Step 2 square; press. At this point each A Unit should measure 4-1/2 x 12-1/2-inches.

A Unit
Make 12

Step 4 Sew Step 2 squares to the side edges of a 4-1/2-inch **BEIGE #2** square; press. <u>At this point each B Unit should measure 4-1/2 x 12-1/2-inches.</u>

B Unit
Make 6

Step 5 Sew A Units to the top/bottom edges of a B Unit; press. <u>At this point each Block B should measure 12-1/2-inches square.</u>

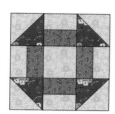

Block B
Make 6

Quilt Center

Cutting

From GOLD PRINT:
- Cut 6, 2-1/2 x 42-inch strips. From the strips, cut: 17, 2-1/2 x 12-1/2-inch lattice segments

From GREEN FLORAL:
- Cut 1, 2-1/2 x 42-inch strip. From the strip, cut: 6, 2-1/2-inch lattice post squares

Quilt Center Assembly

Step 1 For each lattice strip, sew together 3 of the 2-1/2 x 12-1/2-inch **GOLD** lattice segments and 2 of the 2-1/2-inch **GREEN FLORAL** lattice post squares. Press the seam allowances toward the lattice segments. <u>At this point each lattice strip should measure 2-1/2 x 40-1/2-inches.</u>

Make 3 lattice strips

Step 2 Referring to the quilt diagram for block placement, lay out the A Blocks, B Blocks, and the remaining 2-1/2 x 12-1/2-inch **GOLD** lattice segments in 4 horizontal rows. Each block row will have 3 blocks and 2 lattice segments. Sew the pieces together in

each row. Press the seam allowances toward the lattice segments. <u>At this point each block row should measure 12-1/2 x 40-1/2-inches.</u>

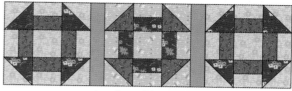

Make 2 block rows

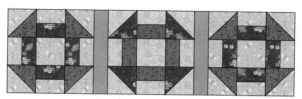

Make 2 block rows

Step 3 Referring to the quilt diagram for placement, sew the block rows and lattice strips together; press the seam allowances in one direction. <u>At this point the quilt center should measure 40-1/2 x 54-1/2-inches.</u>

Borders

Note: *The yardage given allows for the border strips to be cut on the crosswise grain. Diagonally piece the strips as needed, referring to **Diagonal Piecing** instructions on page 159. Read through **Border** instructions on page 158 for general instructions on adding borders.*

Cutting

From GREEN PRINT:
- Cut 5, 2-1/2 x 42-inch inner border strips
- Cut 4 more 2-1/2 x 42-inch strips for checkerboard border

From GREEN DIAGONAL CHECK:
- Cut 7, 4-1/2 x 42-inch middle border strips
- Cut 4, 2-1/2 x 42-inch strips for checkerboard border

From PURPLE FLORAL:
- Cut 10, 10-1/2 x 42-inch outer border strips

Assembling and Attaching the Borders

Step 1   Attach the 2-1/2-inch wide **GREEN PRINT** inner border strips.

Step 2   Attach the 4-1/2-inch wide **GREEN DIAGONAL CHECK** middle border strips.

Step 3   Aligning long edges, sew together the 2-1/2 x 42-inch **GREEN PRINT** and **GREEN DIAGONAL CHECK** strips in pairs; press. Make a total of 4 strip sets. Cut the strip sets into segments.

Crosscut 62, 2-1/2-inch wide segments

Step 4   For the top/bottom checkerboard borders, sew together 13 of the Step 3 segments; press. Make a total of 2 checkerboard border strips. Sew the borders to the quilt center; press.

Step 5   For the left checkerboard border, sew together 18 of the segments, remove a 2-1/2-inch **GREEN DIAGONAL CHECK** square from 1 end; press. Sew the checkerboard border to the quilt center; press.

Step 6   For the right checkerboard border, sew together 18 of the segments, remove a 2-1/2-inch **GREEN PRINT** square from 1 end; press. Sew the checkerboard border to the quilt center; press.

Step 7   Attach the 10-1/2-inch wide **PURPLE FLORAL** outer border strips.

Putting It All Together

Cut the 5-1/3 yard length of backing fabric in half crosswise to make 2, 2-2/3 yard lengths. Refer to *Finishing the Quilt* on page 159 for complete instructions.

Binding

Cutting

From **GREEN PRINT:**
   • Cut 9, 2-3/4 x 42-inch strips

Sew the binding to the quilt using a 3/8-inch seam allowance. This measurement will produce a 1/2-inch wide finished double binding. Refer to *Binding* and *Diagonal Piecing* on page 159 for complete instructions.

Churn Dash Delight Quilt

76 x 90-inches

General Instructions

Getting Started

Yardage is based on 42-inch wide fabric. If your fabric is wider or narrower, it will affect the amount of necessary strips you need to cut in some patterns, and of course, it will affect the amount of fabric you have left over. Generally, Thimbleberries® patterns allow for a little extra fabric so you can confidently cut your pattern pieces with ease.

A rotary cutter, mat, and wide clear plastic ruler with 1/8-inch markings are needed tools in attaining accuracy. A beginner needs good tools just as an experienced quilt maker needs good equipment. A 24 x 36-inch rotary cutting mat board is a good size to own. It will easily accommodate the average quilt fabrics and will aid in accurate cutting. The acrylic ruler you purchase should be at least 6 x 24-inches and easy to read. Do not purchase a smaller ruler to save money. The large size will be invaluable to your quilt making success.

It is often recommended to prewash and press fabrics to test for colorfastness and possible shrinkage. If you choose to prewash, wash in cool water and dry in a cool to moderate dryer. Industry standards actually suggest that line drying is best. Shrinkage is generally very minimal and usually is not a concern. A good way to test your fabric for both shrinkage and colorfastness is to cut a 3-inch square of fabric. Soak the fabric in a white bowl filled with water. Squeeze the water out of the fabric and press it dry on a piece of muslin. If the fabric is going to release color, it will do so either in the water or when it is pressed dry. Remeasure the 3-inch fabric square to see if it has changed size considerably (more than 1/4-inch). If it has, wash, dry, and press the entire yardage. This little test could save you hours in prewashing and pressing.

Read instructions thoroughly before beginning a project. Each step will make more sense to you when you have a general overview of the whole process. Take one step at a time and follow the illustrations. They will often make more sense to you than the words. Take "baby steps" so you don't get overwhelmed by the entire process.

When working with flannel and other loosely woven fabrics, always prewash and dry. These fabrics almost always shrink more.

For piecing, place right sides of the fabric pieces together and use 1/4-inch seam allowances throughout the entire quilt unless otherwise specifically stated in the directions. An accurate seam allowance is the most important part of the quilt making process after accurately cutting. All the directions are based on accurate 1/4-inch seam allowances. It is very important to check your sewing machine to see what position your fabric should be to get accurate seams. To test, use a piece of 1/4-inch graph paper, stitch along the quarter inch line as if the paper were fabric. Make note of where the edge of the paper lines up with your presser foot or where it lines up on the throat plate of your machine. Many quilters place a piece of masking tape on the throat plate to help guide the edge of the fabric. Now test your seam allowance on fabric. Cut 2, 2-1/2-inch squares, place right sides together and stitch along one edge. Press seam allowances in one direction and measure. <u>At this point the unit should measure 2-1/2 x 4-1/2-inches.</u> If it does not, adjust your stitching guidelines and test again. Seam allowances are included in the cutting sizes given in this book.

Pressing is the third most important step in quilt making. As a general rule, you should never cross a stitched seam with another seam unless it has been pressed. Therefore, every time you stitch a seam, it needs to be pressed before adding another piece. Often, it will feel like you press as much as you sew, and often that is true. It is very important that you press and not iron the seams. Pressing is a firm, up-and-down motion that will flatten the seams but not distort the piecing. Ironing is a back-and-forth motion and will stretch and distort the small pieces. Most quilters use steam to help the pressing process. The moisture does help and will not distort the shapes as long as the pressing motion is used.

An old-fashioned rule is to press seam allowances in one direction, toward the darker fabric. Often, background fabrics are light in color and pressing toward the darker fabric prevents the seam allowances from showing through to the right side. Pressing seam allowances in one direction is thought to create a stronger seam. Also, for ease in hand quilting, the quilting lines should fall on the side of the seam which is opposite the seam allowance. As you piece quilts, you will find these "rules" to be helpful but not neccesarily always appropriate. Sometimes seams need to be pressed in the opposite direction so the seams of different units will fit together more easily,

which quilters refer to as seams "nesting" together. When sewing together two units with opposing seam allowances, use the tip of your seam ripper to gently guide the units under your presser foot. Sometimes it is necessary to re-press the seams to make the units fit together nicely. Always try to achieve the least bulk in one spot and accept that no matter which way you press, it may be a little tricky and it could be a little bulky.

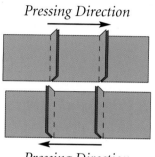

Pressing Direction

Pressing Direction

Squaring Up Blocks

To square up your blocks, first check the seam allowances. This is usually where the problem is, and it is always best to alter within the block rather than trim the outer edges. Next, make sure you have pressed accurately. Sometimes a block can become distorted by ironing instead of pressing.

To trim up block edges, use one of many clear plastic squares available on the market. Determine the center of the block; mark with a pin. Lay the square over the block and align as many perpendicular and horizontal lines as you can to the seams in your block. This will indicate where the block is off.

Do not trim all off on one side; this usually results in real distortion of the pieces in the block and the block design. Take a little off all sides until the block is square. When assembling many blocks, it is necessary to make sure *all* are the same size.

Tools and Equipment

Making beautiful quilts does not require a large number of specialized tools or expensive equipment. My list of favorites is short and sweet and includes the things I use over and over again because they are always accurate and dependable.

I find a long acrylic ruler indispensable for accurate rotary cutting. The ones I like most are an Omnigrid® 6 x 24-inch grid acrylic ruler for cutting long strips and squaring up fabrics and quilt tops and a Masterpiece 45, 8 x 24-inch ruler for cutting 6- to 8-inch wide borders. I sometimes tape together two 6 x 24-inch acrylic rulers for cutting borders up to 12-inches wide.

A 15-inch Omnigrid® square acrylic ruler is great for squaring up individual blocks and corners of a quilt top, for cutting strips up to 15 inches wide or long, and for trimming side and corner triangles.

I think the markings on my 24 x 36-inch Olfa® rotary cutting mat stay visible longer than on other mats, and the lines are fine and accurate.

The largest size Olfa® rotary cutter cuts through many layers of fabric easily, and it isn't cumbersome to use. The 2-1/2-inch blade slices through three layers of backing, batting, and a quilt top like butter.

An 8-inch pair of Gingher shears is great for cutting out appliqué templates and cutting fabric from a bolt or fabric scraps.

I keep a pair of 5-1/2-inch Gingher scissors by my sewing machine so it is handy for both machine work and handwork. This size is versatile and sharp enough to make large and small cuts equally well.

My Grabbit magnetic pin cushion has a surface that is large enough to hold lots of straight pins and a magnet strong enough to keep them securely in place.

Silk pins are long and thin, which means they won't leave large holes in your fabric. I like them because they increase accuracy in pinning pieces or blocks together and it is easy to press over silk pins as well.

For pressing individual pieces, blocks, and quilt tops, I use an 18 x 48-inch sheet of plywood covered with several layers of cotton fiberfill and topped with a layer of muslin stapled to the back. The 48-inch length allows me to press an entire width of fabric at one time without the need to reposition it, and the square ends are better than tapered ends on an ironing board for pressing finished quilt tops.

Rotary Cutting

SAFETY FIRST! The blades of a rotary cutter are very sharp and need to be for accurate cutting. Look at a variety of cutters to find one that feels good in your hand. All quality cutters have a safety mechanism to "close" the cutting blade when not in use. After each cut and before laying the rotary cutter down, close the blade. Soon this will become second nature to you and will prevent dangerous accidents. Always keep cutters out of the sight of children. Rotary cutters are very tempting to fiddle with when they are laying around. When your blade is dull or nicked, change it. Damaged blades do not cut accurately and require extra effort that can also result in slipping and injury. Also, always cut away from yourself for safety.

Fold the fabric in half lengthwise matching the selvage edges.

"Square off" the ends of your fabric before measuring and cutting pieces. This means that the cut edge of the fabric must be exactly perpendicular to the folded edge which creates a 90° angle. Align the folded and selvage edges of the fabric with the lines on the cutting board,

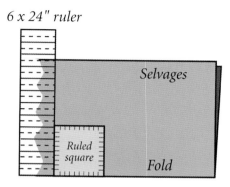

6 x 24" ruler

and place a ruled square on the fold. Place a 6 x 24-inch ruler against the side of the square to get a 90° angle. Hold the ruler in place, remove the square, and cut along the edge of the ruler. If you are left-handed, work from the other end of the fabric. Use the lines on your cutting board to help line up fabric, but not to measure and cut strips. Use a ruler for accurate cutting, always checking to make sure your fabric is lined up with horizontal and vertical lines on the ruler.

Cutting Strips

When cutting strips or rectangles, cut on the crosswise grain. Strips can then be cut into squares or smaller rectangles.

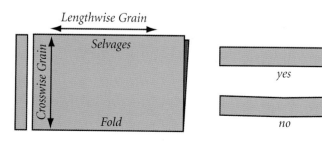

If your strips are not straight after cutting a few of them, refold the fabric, align the folded and selvage edges with the lines on the cutting board, and "square off" the edge again by trimming to straighten, and begin cutting.

Trimming Side and Corner Triangles

In projects with side and corner triangles, the instructions have you cut side and corner triangles larger than needed. This will allow you to square up the quilt and eliminates the frustration of ending up with precut side and corner triangles that don't match the size of your pieced blocks.

To cut triangles, first cut squares. The project directions will tell you what size to make the squares and whether to cut them in half to make two triangles

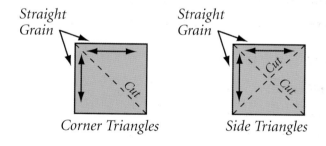

or to cut them in quarters to make four triangles, as shown in the diagrams. This cutting method will give you side triangles that have the straight grain on the outside edges of the quilt. This is a very important part of quilt making that will help stabilize your quilt center.

Helpful Hints for Sewing with Flannel

Always prewash and machine dry flannel. This will prevent severe shrinkage after the quilt is made. Some flannels shrink more than others. For this reason, we have allowed approximately 1/4 yard extra for each fabric under the fabric requirements. Treat the more heavily napped side of solid flannels as the right side of the fabric.

Because flannel stretches more than other cotton calicos and because the nap makes them thicker, the quilt design should be simple. Let the fabric and color make the design statement.

Consider combining regular cotton calicos with flannels. The different textures complement each other nicely.

Use a 10 to 12 stitches per inch setting on your machine. A 1/4-inch seam allowance is also recommended for flannel piecing.

When sewing triangle-pieced squares together, take extra care not to stretch the diagonal seam. Trim off the points from the seam allowances to eliminate bulk.

Press gently to prevent stretching pieces out of shape.

Check block measurements as you progress. "Square up" the blocks as needed. Flannel will shift and it is easy to end up with blocks that are misshapen. If you trim and measure as you go, you are more likely to have accurate blocks. If you notice a piece of flannel is stretching more than the others, place it on the bottom when stitching on the machine. The natural action of the feed dogs will help prevent it from stretching.

Before stitching pieces, strips, or borders together, pin often to prevent fabric from stretching and moving. When stitching longer pieces together, divide the pieces into quarters and pin. Divide into even smaller sections to get more control.

Use a lightweight batting to prevent the quilt from becoming too heavy.

Cutting Triangles from Squares

Cutting accurate triangles can be intimidating for beginners, but a clear plastic ruler, rotary cutter, and cutting mat are all that are needed to make perfect triangles. The cutting instructions often direct you to cut strips, then squares, and then triangles.

Sewing Layered Strips Together

When you are instructed to layer strips, right sides together, and sew, you need to take some precautions. Gently lay a strip on top of another, carefully lining up the raw edges. Pressing the strips together will hold them together nicely, and a few pins here and there will also help. Be careful not to stretch the strips as you sew them together.

Rod Casing or Sleeve to Hang Quilts

To hang wall quilts, attach a casing that is made of the same fabric as the quilt back. Attach this casing at the top of the quilt, just below the binding. Often, it is helpful to attach a second casing at the bottom of the quilt so you can insert a dowel into it which will help weight the quilt and make it hang free of ripples.

To make a rod casing or "sleeve," cut enough strips of fabric equal to the width of the quilt plus 2-inches for side hems. Generally, 6-inch wide strips will accommodate most rods. If you are using a rod with a larger diameter, increase the width of the strips.

Seam the strips together to get the length needed; press. Fold the strip in half lengthwise, wrong sides together. Stitch the long raw edges together with a 1/4-inch seam allowance. Center the seam on the backside of the sleeve; press. The raw edges of the seam will be concealed when the sleeve is stitched to the back of the quilt. Turn under both of the short raw edges; press and stitch to hem the ends. The final measurement should be about 1/2-inch from the quilt edges.

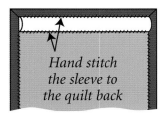

Hand stitch the sleeve to the quilt back

Pin the sleeve to the back of the quilt so the top edge of the sleeve is just below the binding. Hand stitch the top edge of the sleeve in place, then the bottom edge. Make sure to knot and secure your stitches at each end of the sleeve to make sure it will not pull away from the quilt with use. Slip the rod into the casing. If your wall quilt is not directional, making a sleeve for the bottom edge will allow you to turn your quilt end to end to relieve the stress at the top edge. You could also slip a dowel into the bottom sleeve to help anchor the lower edge of the wall quilt.

Choosing a Quilt Design

Quilting is such an individual process that it is difficult to recommend designs for each quilt. There are hundreds of quilting stencils available at quilt shops. (Templates are used generally for appliqué shapes; stencils are used for marking quilting designs.)

There are a few suggestions that may help you decide how to quilt your project, depending on how much time you would like to spend quilting. Many quilters now use professional long-arm quilting machines or hire someone skilled at running these machines to do the quilting. This, of course, frees up more time to piece.

Quilting Suggestions

Repeat one of the design elements in the quilt as part of the quilting design.

Two or three parallel rows of echo quilting outside an appliqué piece will highlight the shape.

Stipple or meander quilting behind a feather or central motif will make the primary design more prominent.

Look for quilting designs that will cover two or more borders, rather than choosing separate designs for each individual border.

Quilting in the ditch of seams is an effective way to get a project quilted without a great deal of time marking the quilt.

Marking the Quilting Design

When marking the quilt top, use a marking tool that will be visible on the quilt fabric and yet will be easy enough to remove. Always test your marking tool on a scrap of fabric before marking the entire quilt.

Along with a multitude of commercial marking tools available, you may find that very thin slivers of hand soap (Dial, Ivory, etc.) work really well for marking medium to dark color fabrics. The thin lines of soap show up nicely and they are easily removed by simply rubbing gently with a piece of like-colored fabric.

Hints and Helps for Pressing Strip Sets

When sewing strips of fabric together for strip sets, it is important to press the seam allowances nice and flat, usually to the darker fabric. Be careful not to stretch as you press, causing a "rainbow effect." This will affect the accuracy and shape of the pieces cut from the strip set. I like to press on the wrong side first and with the strips perpendicular to the ironing board. Then I flip the piece over and press on the right side to prevent little pleats from forming at the seams. Laying the strip set lengthwise on the ironing board seems to encourage the rainbow effect, as shown in the diagram.

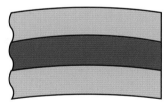

Avoid this rainbow effect

Borders

NOTE: *Cut borders to the width called for. Always cut border strips a few inches longer than needed, just to be safe. Diagonally piece the border strips together as needed.*

1. With pins, mark the center points along all 4 sides of the quilt. For the top and bottom borders, measure the quilt from left to right through the middle.

2. Measure and mark the border lengths and center points on the strips cut for the borders before sewing them on.

3. Pin the border strips to the quilt and stitch a 1/4-inch seam. Press the seam allowances toward the border. Trim off excess border lengths.

Trim away excess fabric

4. For the side borders, measure your quilt from top to bottom, including the borders just added, to determine the length of the side borders.

5. Measure and mark the side border lengths as you did for the top and bottom borders.

6. Pin and stitch the side border strips in place. Press and trim the border strips even with the borders just added.

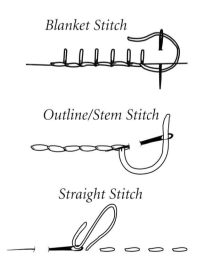

Trim away excess fabric

7. If your quilt has multiple borders, measure, mark, and sew additional borders to the quilt in the same manner.

Decorative Stitches

Blanket Stitch

Outline/Stem Stitch

Straight Stitch

Finishing the Quilt

1. Remove the selvages from the backing fabric. Sew the long edges together and press. Trim the backing and batting so they are 2-inches to 4-inches larger than the quilt top.

2. Mark the quilt top for quilting. Layer the backing, batting, and quilt top. Baste the 3 layers together and quilt.

3. When quilting is complete, remove basting. Hand baste all 3 layers together a scant 1/4-inch from the edge. This hand basting keeps the layers from shifting and prevents puckers from forming when adding the binding. Trim excess batting and backing fabric even with the edge of the quilt top. Add the binding as shown below.

Binding and Diagonal Piecing

Diagonal Piecing

Stitch diagonally *Trim to 1/4-inch seam allowance* *Press seam open*

1. Diagonally piece the binding strips. Fold the strip in half lengthwise, wrong sides together, and press.

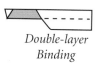

Double-layer Binding

2. Unfold and trim one end at a 45° angle. Turn under the edge 3/8-inch and press. Refold the strip.

Fold line

3. With raw edges of the binding and quilt top even, stitch with a 3/8-inch seam allowance, starting 2-inches from the angled end.

4. Miter the binding at the corners. As you approach a corner of the quilt, stop sewing 3/8-inch from the corner of the quilt.

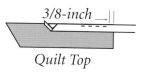

3/8-inch

Quilt Top

5. Clip the threads and remove the quilt from under the presser foot. Flip the binding strip up and away from the quilt, then fold the binding down even with the raw edge of the quilt. Begin sewing at the upper edge. Miter all 4 corners in this manner.

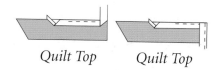

Quilt Top   *Quilt Top*

6. Trim the end of the binding so it can be tucked inside of the beginning binding about 1/2-inch. Finish stitching the seam.

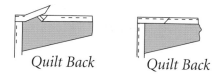

Quilt Back   *Quilt Back*

7. Turn the folded edge of the binding over the raw edges and to the back of the quilt so that the stitching line does not show. Hand sew the binding in place, folding in the mitered corners as you stitch.

 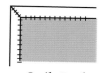

Quilt Back   *Quilt Back*   *Quilt Back*

Mary Lou Herndon
202 193rd St
Smithville MO 64089-9162